TRANSMONTANUS 23

Mudflat Dreaming

Published by New Star Books

Other books in the Transmontanus series

1. A GHOST IN THE WATER *Terry Glavin*
2. CHIWID *Sage Birchwater*
3. THE GREEN SHADOW *Andrew Struthers*
4. HIGH SLACK *Judith Williams*
5. ALL POSSIBLE WORLDS *Justine Brown*
6. RED LAREDO BOOTS *Theresa Kishkan*
7. A VOICE GREAT WITHIN US *Charles Lillard with Terry Glavin*
8. GUILTY OF EVERYTHING *John Armstrong*
9. KOKANEE: THE REDFISH AND THE KOOTENAY BIOREGION *Don Gayton*
10. THE CEDAR SURF *Grant Shilling*
11. DYNAMITE STORIES *Judith Williams*
12. THE OLD RED SHIRT *Yvonne Mearns Klan*
13. MARIA MAHOI OF THE ISLANDS *Jean Barman*
14. BASKING SHARKS *Scott Wallace and Brian Gisborne*
15. CLAM GARDENS *Judith Williams*
16. WRECK BEACH *Carellin Brooks*
17. STRANGER WYCOTT'S PLACE *John Schreiber*
18. OFF THE HIGHWAY *Mette Bach*
19. STRANGER ON A STRANGE ISLAND *Grant Buday*
20. STURGEON REACH *Terry Glavin & Ben Parfitt*
21. GARDENS AFLAME *Maleea Acker*
22. CULTURE GAP: TOWARDS A NEW WORLD IN THE YALAKOM VALLEY *Judith Plant*

Mudflat Dreaming

WATERFRONT BATTLES AND THE SQUATTERS

WHO FOUGHT THEM IN 1970S VANCOUVER

Jean Walton

TRANSMONTANUS / NEW STAR BOOKS VANCOUVER

For Nancy and Jack,
with a salute to those A-frame days
on the King George Highway

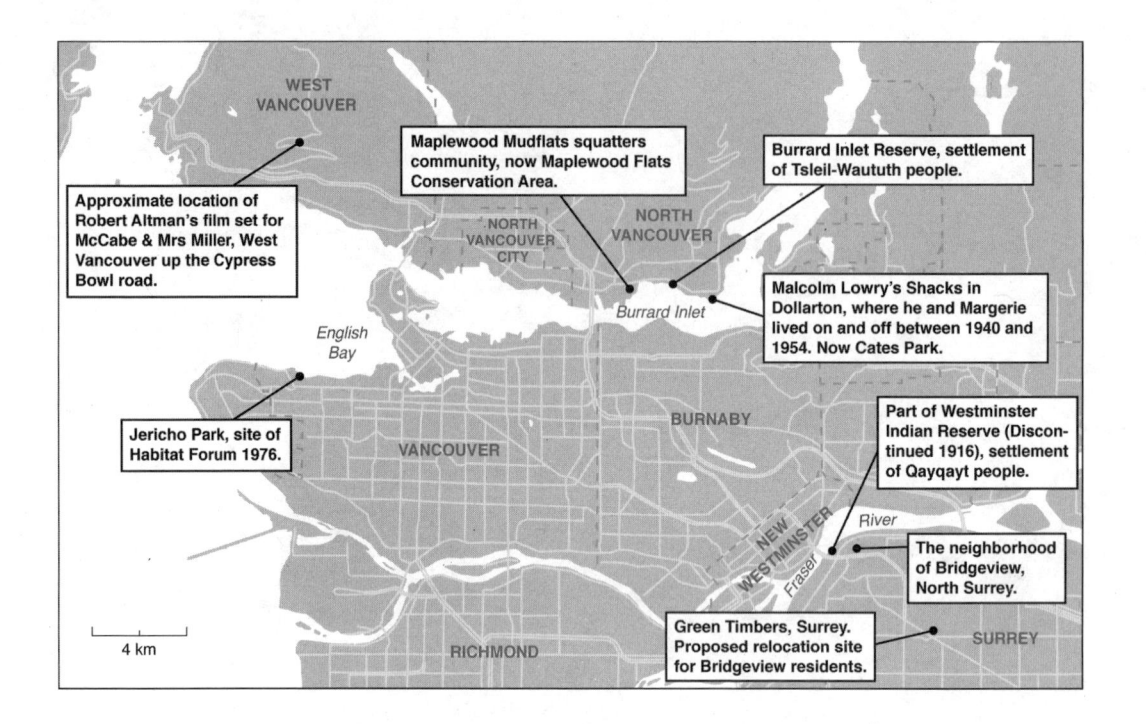

Map of Vancouver and environs, showing Maplewood Mudflats squatters site, Bridgeview neighborhood, MCCABE & MRS. MILLER *set,* Habitat Forum *at Jericho Beach and other locations.*

This land is your land, this land is my land
From California to New York Island.

How often I sang this song, in school, at summer camp, in the family car as we drove through the Redwood Forest, or with our cousins down near the Gulf Stream waters. How easy it was to learn that all of "America the Beautiful," its spacious skies, its amber waves of grain, was made for you and me. It seemed like almost every song I learned in childhood affirmed a proud claim to a tract of territory — like Boulder, Colorado, where the columbines grow, or the hills the greenest green in Seattle — vast or local, hilly or flat, and most of all, smiled upon by a deity, as though to bless our attachment to it.

This is not to say I was a particularly patriotic child, but just that I must have come to take for granted a sense of belonging to a land, and its belonging to me, by the time I turned thirteen and we moved to Canada. Only then, when a classmate sneered at my Yankee origins, did I begin to feel the mildest version of what it might mean to live as a stranger in alien territory — and thus to understand that the crossing of a border was no inconsequential thing. This might have been my father's home and native land, but it was hardly mine — or rather, I was going to have to start all over again if I were to embrace this latest bit of mud as the home base from which I was to launch a new life.

I was what you might call a teenage ex-pat, unwillingly displaced in 1970 to live just across the border near Vancouver, on a strip of highway where my grandparents had bought a motel a few years before, which we were now taking over for them. My father was returning to this True North Strong and Free and, more specifically, to what had been hailed by his parents as an exciting new business opportunity, given the hordes that would surely pour into British Columbia for fishing vacations and skiing holidays, or even to settle in the rapidly developing suburban tracts that were spreading out along the Fraser Valley, from Vancouver itself to Langley or even Mission, 40 miles upriver.

I recount this bit of autobiography as a way into a story I want to tell — not about my own family's occupation of a liminal frontier near Canada's Emerald City, but of two settlements, one on the south bank of the Fraser, very near to our own commercial strip on the King George Highway; the other almost directly northwest of us as the crow flies, on the north shore of Vancouver's Burrard Inlet, just off the Dollarton Highway. I've come to think of these as twinned communities, both on the water's edge, both the sites of dramatic territorial conflicts, both harbingers in their way of the almost unbearable situation ordinary Vancouverites find themselves in today.

It's difficult to know how to enter this tale of land contestation, uncertain as I am of whom I'm addressing. Is it Canadians, and more specifically Vancouverites, who already know the story — or at least half of it — as a legend they keep telling themselves in a nostalgic tribute to a cherished pre-modern past? Or is it Americans, who know little of Canada and practically nothing of its westernmost outposts, often picturing their northern neighbor as comprising vast snowy prairies — an impression that's accurate when applied to Manitoba, where my father grew up, but hardly appropriate for the rain-soaked and mountainous West Coast, which (as I inform my friends) is more like Seattle — mild and verdant.

To my Vancouver audience, then, I call upon you to accompany me in this story, as though we are telling it together to an ill-informed American populace. I cannot count myself as one of you anymore, and perhaps I never could, despite the decade I spent on British Columbian soil. But maybe my distance in time and geography from my one-time stomping grounds permits me to address the story to Vancouverites as well, both the part you never tire of hearing, as well as the other part you've forgotten. It's about shacks on a shoreline, drawn-out battles with local mayors, avid squatters of literary fame, and unwitting squatters of working-class obscurity. It's about flows and seepage, downpours and upsurges, salt tides and dirty ditches and alarming coliform counts. It's about the family you left behind, the family you made with your friends, the family that you tried, so hard, to save from eviction. But it's also about those long-gone 1970s romances: a utopia not so much "off" the grid as nestled in with its detritus; the idea of free children, running wild and unfettered; the image of the countercultural artist who needs a supportive woman by his side; the pure ore of doing one's own thing, crafting with your own hands, and crossing paths with just the right woman of the night, with her heart of gold.

It's about the glitter I found while panning in the past of my West Coast adolescence forty years after the fact. You know what it's like. You have just one little bitty question, maybe you're hoping to find someone's family album with fading snapshots of the very block on which you lived at one time, or you want to remind yourself of what the corner up the hill from your house looked like before the SkyTrain came through and rearranged the landscape. Just that one thing, and you know where to start sifting, too, with that best of all mining tools for excavating the past: the internet. But next thing you know you've gone down a rabbit hole that's more like an endless mine shaft, and who knows when you'll find your way out again.

Oh sure, you've travelled back to your hometown in real life, all the way across the continent, across the border, to visit your sister and brother as the nieces and nephews grow up. And every time you show up, you are struck by how tenacious that pull of nostalgia is. You know what it's like — every time you make that return pilgrimage, it still retains about it a distinct whiff of the past; every time you turn your rented car up a remembered street, or look across the Fraser at the mountain range that always seemed like an ancient woman to you, finally giving up, exhausted, just lying down on her back; every hour you spend in the drizzle that seems to materialize in the air rather than descend from the uniform grey of the low-lying cloud cover — it all seems imbued somehow with an aura of the once known but now abandoned.

Because abandoned by you.

When you visit, your sister and brother have no idea you are experiencing this, despite your shared childhoods. Because they never left, these streets, these shaggy cedars, these glistening lawns and uniform strip malls have the banal feel of the contemporaneous day-to-day. Nothing special. But to you, coming back to the place is always a return to the past. You can't get to the bottom of this odd sensation by being in the present of the place that is a past to you. That's why you turn to the archives of that past, if not to dissipate the nostalgia, at least to better acquaint yourself with its contours.

In my case, the expedition to find a '70s Vancouver led me almost immediately to three short documentary films, antiquated fragments of a former era, that were as precious for their vivid depiction of the time and place in which they were made as for the urgent arguments they wished to impress upon their original audiences.

One was dimly familiar to me — had I seen it before? Or maybe it's just that it featured the same small-time politicians I had come to know while working as a teenage photographer for our local weekly newspaper, the *Surrey–Delta Messenger*. This was *Some People Have to Suffer*, a documentary by Canada's National Film Board (NFB) about the plight of a working-class neighbourhood barely a mile away from our motel, at the bottom of the King George Highway as it arrived at the banks of the Fraser River. Here, residents living on the flats of the flood plain, in a small enclave called Bridgeview, could be found petitioning Surrey city council for basic amenities to upgrade their aging infrastructure. With its images of ramshackle houses set amongst salvage yards and lumber mills, children with lunch pails sprayed by passing trucks, and mealy-mouthed Surrey mayor Bill Vander Zalm taking a drag from his cigarette as he wonders whether it might be better to relocate everyone and just industrialize the whole area, the film brought back to me vague recollections of the insinuations of my new classmates, who despised the lowlifes living in that contemptible corner "down the hill," so out of place in a municipality that fancied itself as the new suburbia for the middle class. The effect this film had on me was downright Proustian, with its travelling shots of contaminated ditchwater, the orange girders of the bridge across the Fraser, the tumbledown houses fronted by weedy ditches, constant downpours, and shouting matches in the crowded council chambers. I could almost feel the clammy slap of the bellbottoms at my ankles, smell the stench after the latest rainfall. Thanks to the NFB, I was restored almost wholesale to those overcast years we spent on the King George Highway in Canada's largest, but maybe most maligned, municipality: Surrey.

'From one clogged culvert to another' – Bridgeview ditch. Some People Have to Suffer

The other two films, *Mudflats Living*, an NFB production, and *Livin' on the Mud*, an independent film by a documentarist from Washington State, also featured scenes of conflict between residents and a local mayor, between livability and commercial development, between the mud of natural abundance and the cement of civic improvement. But in this case the films paid lyrical tribute to a small squatter community of artists, craftsmen, countercultural types, living in a hodgepodge of wooden shacks on piles, raising them above the high-water level as the tides washed in and out along the shore. These people, the latest wave of a long history of squatters along the city's waterways, lived on an estuary, the Maplewood Mudflats, where McCartney Creek and its tributaries, coming down from the North Shore Mountains, met the salt tides washing in from the inlet that divides Vancouver from its nearest suburb to the north. Here you could erect your dwelling in the liminal space where municipal property met the waters regulated by the National Harbours Board, the mean tide line, neither far enough out to interfere with the shipping traffic, nor close enough to count as dry land.

The conflict was similar: how long would they be permitted to remain in their houses before forced eviction made way for municipal development schemes? While the residents in Bridgeview longed for the amenities their upland neighbours enjoyed, the hippies on the Maplewood Mudflats seemed to spurn the trappings of suburban life — if they had "running water," it was borrowed through a hose stretching out to the beach from a friendly ratepayer's house, or collected from one of the springs flowing off the mountain, not purchased through the local tax structure. As for sewage, well, you couldn't really tell from the films, but it seemed that the tides washed everything clean at least twice a day, nature taking care of all the dwellers along this stretch of primeval mud. Some people chose squatting, like these artisans and exiles from the "rat race" as my father called it; others, like our neighbours down in Bridgeview, had squatting thrust upon them. For it all amounts to the same thing: to live, from one day to the next, with the threat of eviction hanging over you.

As a teenager, I had been unaware of the Maplewood Mudflats squatters — but now, having found the films, I was captivated by them. No doubt they had the same allure for me that they have had for Vancouver audiences in the decades that followed the films' initial release in the early '70s — something about the earnest idealism, the rustic aesthetic that made a virtue of dilapidation, the ironic contrast of the coastal wildlife with the infernal smokestacks of the refinery just across the inlet.

I set out to investigate further. I wanted to follow through on some of the meanings gestured at in these short films, which were like reports from a kind of battlefield. But I also sought to know more about the circumstances that gave rise to them; what was it about these particular Northwest living conditions that attracted the documentarist's eye and seemed worth preserving in this era when so many were trying to democratize the power of the moving image? Where were they today, those tenacious residents of Vancouver's waterfront fringes, to the north of the city and south of the river? What had happened after the ambiguous conclusions depicted by each filmmaker — human dwellings swamped by rising floods or enveloped by raging flames? And if one extended the timeline even further back, by as little as a few decades, what hidden story might emerge from these squabbles over land use within a West Coast settler society?

The Forest Path to the Spring

While I was acquainting my middle-aged self with these idealized denizens of mudflat utopia, it was only a matter of time before I discovered their august predecessor, the most famous of Vancouver's squatters on the North Shore, though his tenancy there had been two decades earlier. In the late 1940s and '50s, expatriate British writer Malcolm Lowry had lived with his wife, Margerie, a little farther up the inlet in what is now Cates Park, but was then a string of fishermen's cabins, also built on piles, near the one-time mill town of Dollarton, which he fictionalized with the legendary name "Eridanus." Eridanus, the mythical Greek river of life and death, is also a serpentine constellation and so was, for Lowry's purposes, the perfect name for his squatters village, linking earthly water with celestial patterns, this world with the other. Here Lowry completed *Under the Volcano*, the only novel for which he is universally known, a modernist classic made into a movie by John Huston in the mid-'80s.

I hungrily read his story "The Forest Path to the Spring," reputed to document most directly the years he spent as a squatter during and after the war — he called his life there a kind of honeymoon without end. Lowry's story seemed the perfect fantasy space through which to explore what is so seductive about the squatter's life, seductive for the artist and his faithful, uncomplaining helpmeet, who prepares his meals while he labours at his compositions all day, or feeds him descriptive lines about the frost in the morning while she lights the fire and puts on the coffee as he luxuriates a little longer in their warm bed. That's the life I'd lead, the simple life, kept simple by the free labour freely given by a devoted companion, the Margerie to my Malcolm, the Alice B to my Gertrude.

It might be that what I love most about Lowry's "Forest Path to the Spring" is not the North Shore setting, of which it offers such a thickly satisfying description, nor its cloying fictional portrait of marital bliss that, if I'm honest, resonates with me in spite of myself, since I, too, would depict my daily life with my partner as a honeymoon without end, an intimacy in a charmed circle of three — herself, myself, and our little cat — enduring for many years beyond what I would have thought possible, so that, were I a believer, I might ask, as Lowry's narrator does, "My God, why have you given this to us?" which for the faithful or the atheist alike is just another way of expressing astonishment at one's unexpected good luck, as though uttering the question will, like a magic spell, ward off or at least postpone the certainty of mortality. No, what I love most perhaps is the shape of the narrative, its refolding back into itself, its recursive return to the beginning and re-beginning of the narrator's walk along a path from his shack on the tidal shore to the spring just within the forest, where he would go to fill a canister with water and bring it back each evening, and how each time his walk is described there is a difference, a deeper resonance, until it turns out that the physical act of fetching the water accretes within itself the very workings of the narrator's own thinking, feeling, fearing, composing.

Lowry's story of the forest path to the spring is not the most characteristic example of his work, reading, as it does, more like a Canadian *Walden* than the tormented hellish descents of his other fiction, and so a realization about this infamous modernist (how had I not read him before, not until my fifties?), the knowledge of him that everyone else seemed to have already, did not dawn on me until I read his *October Ferry to Gabriola* (completed by Margerie after his death), and then, even later, the novel for which he is best known, *Under the Volcano*. I guess I was moving outward and backward in time, from his obscure writing, set most obviously in the Vancouver I wished to recreate for myself, to that novel most trampled by the common reader, set far south in Mexico and so irrelevant, I assumed, to my own investigations.

Yet not so irrelevant after all. If you've read *Under the Volcano* (listed as number eleven in the Modern Library's 100 Best English-Language Novels of the 20th Century), then you've already encountered an inkling of Lowry's beloved squatter's life on Vancouver's North Shore. It goes by in a flash, though, so you can be forgiven if you don't remember a curious bit of dialogue that takes place when Hugh, brother of the novel's famed alcoholic protagonist Geoffrey Firmin, gives some consideration to the idea that Geoffrey might be better off if he left Mexico altogether and moved to Canada. Hugh is out on horseback with Yvonne, Geoffrey's estranged wife, as the two of them confer, the way family members do, about how best to save the drunkard from himself. Having learned from Yvonne that Vancouver has been proposed as the answer to their problems, Hugh offers up the bit of knowledge he's gleaned about the city: its "Pango Pango quality mingled with sausage and mash and generally a rather Puritan atmosphere," its inhabitants "fast asleep and when you prick them a Union Jack flows out of the hole," the impression you have that no one actually lives there but is merely passing through once they've extracted what they need from it. "Mine the country and quit. Blast the land to pieces, knock down the trees and send them rolling down Burrard Inlet." This is Lowry chiming in through his character here, getting in some barbs at the Vancouver he knows from experience, having moved there himself after Mexico. It's as though the novel is sketching out the path not taken for its hero, the path followed after all by this hero's alter ego, the author. As it turns out, Hugh's advice is not to settle in Vancouver at all, but to

> *go down one of the inlets to some fishing village and buy a shack slap spang on the sea, with only foreshore rights, for, say a hundred dollars. Then live on it this winter for about sixty a month. No phone. No rent. No consulate. Be a squatter. Call on your pioneer ancestors. Water from the well. Chop your own wood.*

Hugh gets completely caught up in this idealized fantasy of the squatters' shack, or, rather, Lowry gets caught up in a documentary description of the very location from which he is laboriously revising *Under the Volcano*, elaborating on the shack's placement "between the forest and the sea," its "pier going down to the water over rough stones," the necessity of going through the woods to the store. Hugh stops speaking to Yvonne at this point, though the descriptive passage continues in italics, as though his and his author's thoughts merge in a single floating stream of consciousness: "The woods will be wet. And occasionally a tree will come crashing down. And sometimes there will be a fog and that fog will freeze. Then your whole forest will become a crystal forest."

The fantasy scenario is dropped, never to be visited again in this novel, since Geoffrey Firmin is summarily extinguished long before he can bring to fruition any escape to a Northwest squatter's cabin. The path never taken. But this passage, and the stories Lowry wrote explicitly set in British Columbia, unfolded for me like a reconnaissance mission, Lowry my scout, bringing back to me, in evocative prose, the setting of the North Shore squatting life in all its twentieth-century incarnations. It is as though Lowry speaks for the squatters of the 1970s as well, or maybe his way of immortalizing the experience on the tidal flats was so powerful that it formed a template for how the squatter's life was always to be lived in this particular locale, with its tidal rhythms, high water lapping against the cabin floor, nights under a starry sky, muddy flats at a morning low tide, a train inching along the opposite side of the inlet, seagulls wheeling in, the oil refinery smoking away like a demonic cathedral, its flame burning through the night, a war in distant lands — the European war in Lowry's day; the Vietnam war as the '60s slid into the '70s. Even the idea that living on the mudflats wasn't, after all, just living, but being "engaged" in a "project."

For this is what "The Forest Path to the Spring" meanders toward all along, this notion of a project. The spring itself, as well as the canister the narrator brings to it, is symbolic of the fragile grace by which the squatting couple are, for the time being, permitted to remain in their beloved cabin on the water. When they first move in, they don't know about the spring; they have to get their drinking water by rowing, at mid-tide level, to a different water source some distance away. And when a NO TRESPASSING sign is erected at that source, they are in despair, thinking they must leave their cabin and move back to the city. No water means no life.

But just as it seems they will have to vacate, one of their fishermen neighbours points out the spring a few hundred yards from their shack, and on the very same day the narrator salvages a ship's canister from the beach, the perfect vessel to carry life's elixir. So every time he makes the trip to the spring, it is an opportunity to reflect on how lucky they are to remain in what seems like an Eden to them, the setting of their young love, of his own physical regeneration after a musician's life of nocturnal debauches.

If there is one thing everyone knows about Malcolm Lowry, it's that he was the writer of alcoholic addiction par excellence, and alcoholism was something I knew a lot about in the 1970s. My father, though perhaps not as epic a drinker as Lowry, came in a close second. So on my first reading of this, my first story by Lowry, I was half on the lookout for veiled references to alcoholism, not knowing yet that he wrote of his addiction quite explicitly in his Mexico novel. The spring, I thought, was a metaphor for drinking somehow, and the narrator's repetitive visits to it the correlative to the drunkard's insatiable thirst, his habitual replenishment. "At dusk, every evening, I used to go through the forest to the spring for water," his story opens, and then "Thereafter at dusk, when the gulls came floating home over the trees, I used to take this canister to the spring," and again, "this is the time I am really thinking of when I say that each evening at dusk I used to go down the path for water." Dusk — the hour at which the most serious drinking always occurred in my own family.

When he happens to meet a mountain lion on the path, and faces it down almost casually, blithely, it occurs to him that he feels no fear because he must have been "already gripped by the anticipation of a so much greater fear that the concrete fact even of a lion had been unable to displace it." What he fears, he decides, is the "soul of a past self," to whom "sleep meant delirium, my thoughts chasing each other down a gulf." If on the path he had been on the lookout for something "on every side, to spring out of our paradise at us," it was

> nothing so much as the embodiment in some frightful animal form of those nameless somnambulisms, guilts, ghouls of past delirium, wounds to other souls and lives, ghosts of actions approximating to murder, even if not my own actions in this life, betrayals of self and I know not what, ready to leap out and destroy me, to destroy us, and our happiness, so that when as if in answer to all this, I saw a mere lion, how could I be afraid?

This "soul of a past self," those "ghouls of past delirium" seem to rise up like phantoms of the destructive alcoholic he used to be — the Geoffrey Firmin heading toward self-annihilation under a Mexican volcano, or the Malcolm Lowry drinking himself into a sordid nightly stupor during those years he spent in Mexico, inventing the consul as his fictional avatar. If the protagonist of "Forest Path" goes through a period when he loses consciousness during his daily journey to the spring, coming back to his senses only when he reaches the safety of the cabin again, it is not, as I had first thought, an allegory of the alcoholic's blackouts. Because it turns out that he has merely been in a kind of artistic trance, working on an ambitious musical project. "Perhaps I have not mentioned my project, or rather what I conceived my project to be," he remarks out of the blue. For although he has at first presented himself as a "retired" jazz musician, no longer officially employed, it turns out that he's been working all along, attempting to compose his musical magnum opus, a symphony that turns into an opera, that he fears he will not be able to finish.

As though to revive the dead consul of *Under the Volcano*, Lowry gives his North Shore hero a happy ending — that is, the satisfaction of completing his musical project. He titles it "The Forest Path to the Spring": the opera standing for the story that narrates the writing of the opera within the story, *mise en abime* of the high modernist portrait of the artist as a young-old squatter. Though there may be "blackouts" in this story, they are not the malignant episodes of the drunkard, but the benign absent-mindedness of the composer who writes in his head as his feet take him home, toting his water to the one who awaits him with open arms.

If Mexico was the scene of the crime of inebriation, the cabin at Dollarton signified the one place in the world that Lowry could survive, he hoped, without drinking massive quantities of alcohol on a daily basis. The story of the forest path to the spring was his tribute to this place, the pure spring water washing the alcohol from his saturated carcass and making it possible for him to complete *Under the Volcano* and to continue with his many other tales that were to be linked together to form a voyage that never ends.

As a would-be writer, my father cherished fantasies of one day finding the perfect shack where he could escape the mundane clamour of our noisy household and finally pursue his own literary aspirations. The cedar A-frame we lived in at the front of the motel — something like a miniature alpine lodge designed to hide the dingy stucco units behind — might have resembled a quaint wooden retreat where the inspired novelist could ply his pen, but crammed as it was with four other people, dog and cat, and all our worldly belongings, and spattered by the gritty spray of the passing highway traffic day and night, it just would not do. As I think about it, maybe it was the mirage of the writer's hideaway that floated through my father's nightly tirades which makes me curious, today, about Lowry's and the other squatters' shacks not so very far away from our motel in Surrey.

Lowry's lyrical portrayal of squatting, as I mentioned earlier, was intended to convey sobriety, marital harmony, and literary productivity. But as seen by his Dollarton neighbours, Lowry still maintained the reputation of an alcoholic of legendary proportions: the kind of drunk who acts foolishly in public because he can't judge the appropriateness of his behaviour. A resident recalled a day when Margerie loaded him up with groceries in the local general store and he suddenly "opened his arms, letting all the groceries fall, making a real mess on the floor. He just stood there while she cleaned it up." Or on another occasion, Margerie tied up their rowboat at the Dollar Mill wharf, and rather than alighting from the boat with her as a sudden downpour began, "he just sat in the bow grinning this damn foolish grin." Or another remembered "seeing him in the middle of summer wearing a fur coat and boots. He was drunk and he scared me." If some people praised the chords he picked out on the piano, to one observer "it just sounded like someone playing in drunkenness." During an evening party, after he'd had a certain amount to drink, the same person reported, "Malcolm would separate himself and, although physically present, he would no longer be a part of the gathering: he'd be on another plane of thought; his conversations would become monologues; if one tried to have a discussion with him one couldn't always keep the connection because his mind would jump and the conversation would become bewildering." She could have been describing my own father, of course, right down to her remark that Lowry was "sensitive about his own feelings," but not too sensitive "about how anybody else was feeling." If his male associates, the literary ones, presented him in a more lenient light, so eager to regard his weakness as a classic "tragic flaw," to make allowances for it because of the prodigious talent that shone through in his writing, then these more jaundiced accounts from the female point of view, impatient at the man's childishness, made me feel, fleetingly, as though I were getting the "true" picture of things. Yes, I thought, reading that he "seemed to think he should be waited on," that's what it's like, sharing the shack with the alcoholic. Don't excuse him; condemn him. Don't even try to understand him; ignore him. He's nothing but a self-absorbed boozer. But then again, this is just the "woman's blame" speaking, by which, to all appearances, the alcoholic is curiously sustained.

Surrey

Nothing makes a city feel more self-satisfied than an unfashionable, shabby, or just plain inferior neighbour that can be made fun of on a regular basis. Think of the much maligned New Jersey in relation to the Big Apple. For Vancouver, the place to joke about is Surrey, and this has been true since the 1970s. If it's not the crime rate, it's the low IQ; if it's not the toxic waste dumps, it's the down-at-heels suburban mindset. And the "Surrey girl" jokes are right out of the X-rated encyclopedia of dumb blonde jokes. It wasn't all of Surrey that got the "belittling" (as my mother used to call my treatment of my younger sister) — the municipality is so vast that it is actually composed of several town centres, parishes, agricultural swathes, golf courses, and resort-like beachfronts. But certain of its semi-commercial, semi-residential corners, like Guildford, Newton, and the farmer town, Cloverdale, have always been fair game for derision. The most susceptible to the jokes, however, was the sector where we lived, Whalley, where the King George Highway intersected with 104th Avenue. Our scruffy little motel, home sometimes to what my father called "transients" who couldn't afford regular houses, sat next to a small-time trucking company, across the street from a similar scruffy motel, and down the highway from the Dell Hotel and Bowling Alley, Roath's Pawn Shop, and the Pink Elephant Laundromat. While my parents seemed to find nothing untoward about this tattered corner of the world, it struck me as a big comedown from some of the places we'd lived before.

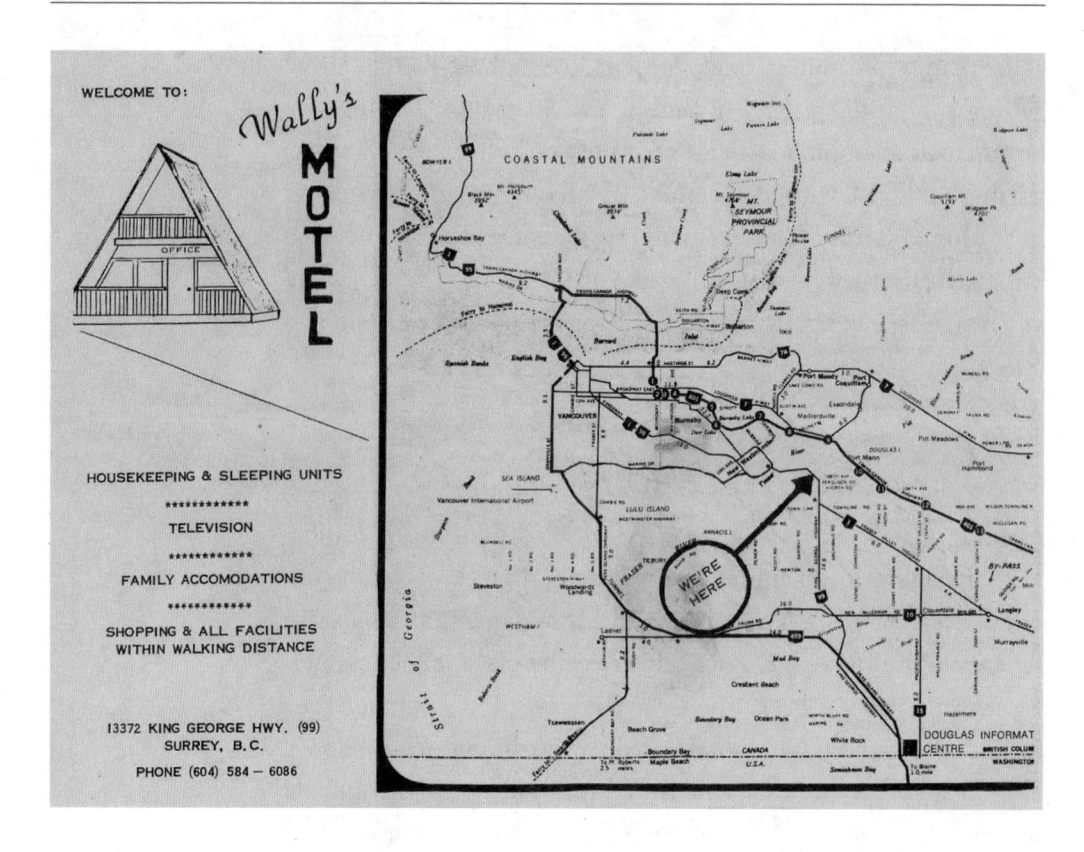

Flyer my father made to advertise our Motel, ca. 1970.

Whalley has transformed in recent years, thanks to the extension of the SkyTrain from Vancouver right out into the heart of Surrey, and the hopeful name change of the King George from "Highway" to "Boulevard," as though to conjure a stately tree-lined thoroughfare rather than a nondescript truck route. The old Whalley Exchange bus loop has also been renamed Surrey Central, and a futuristic steel-and-glass complex, complete with soaring high-rise, was constructed atop the aging Surrey Place Mall, where my classmates got retail jobs when it first opened back in 1972, but which had declined over the ensuing decades, threatening to close down as so many North American malls have done. And yet, even though this corner of the municipality resembles the most postmodern complexes in downtown Vancouver (having been designed, after all, by renowned architect Bing Thom), Surrey is still looked down upon by city dwellers full of contempt. Most recently the bad rep was given a boost by gang warfare in Whalley, and even a few fatal shootings. But the sense that Surrey has more crime than Vancouver proper, or its closer suburbs of Burnaby and New Westminster, has always been around. My one-time junior secondary English teacher told me that he was warned by his college mates, when he took his first teaching post at West Whalley, that he'd for sure get stabbed or mugged. That was back in the 1960s. His comment surprised me; I had not been aware that my school was particularly violent. It wasn't, he told me. But that was what everyone thought about Whalley, back in the day.

My own lack of affection for my new "home town" did not arise from uneasiness about a presumed rampant crime rate. It was rooted in something else altogether.

The line between wilderness and civilization is relative, like the line between water and dry land on tidal mudflats. What really depressed me about this Canadian suburb we had moved to was its absence of sidewalks to clearly delineate the border between one's private home and the public street. Surrey was the first place I'd lived where instead of a sidewalk you found ... a ditch. Once you got off the bit of the King George Highway in front of our motel and moved back into the residential neighbourhoods where my friends lived, you had to walk along the dirt strip where the ditch met the street. Here and there a wooden platform might allow you to cross the ditch into a yard to reach someone's front door, a sort of mini-drawbridge over the moat, but for the most part all I recall are the ditches themselves. Nary a curb in sight, and I found this distressing. Was it because I had learned to take for granted the sidewalks in front of our previous houses, my roller-skating venues of days gone by? The ditches were, to my would-be middle-class sensibility, a sign that we had gone backward in what should have been a forward evolution of our family. Our surroundings were getting uglier; the climate damper; the social possibilities seemingly limited to hockey schedules and pep rallies.

Apparently much of the city of Vancouver itself was still curbless, as it had been twenty years before when, late one night, Malcolm Lowry, who had been visiting friends in the city, went out to bid another guest farewell, then failed to return. When his friends went looking for him, he turned up "in the sewer ditch that ran along the front of the house. I don't know whether he was happily lying in the ditch," said one friend, "but he didn't make any outcries. He had to be fished out and cleaned up. He was quite pitiful at times." The city still had those ditches that ran in front of the houses during the '70s; it wasn't only the Surrey streets that might pose a hazard to the nocturnal drunken misstep.

By the time we crossed the border, Surrey aspired to be the kind of outlying area you move to when you want to fulfill your dream of owning a house, parking your car in your garage, mowing your lawn, fencing your dog in the backyard, and raising your family. That was a lifestyle my parents had sought, before the motel, in our rented houses in Seattle, Boulder, and the Bay Area. In all those cases, sidewalks were involved. But the Surrey version of this suburban residential ideal seemed flawed to me, blemished. As though it was striving to be picture perfect but not succeeding. It wasn't just the lack of curbs that made it raggedy around the edges; it was the residential architecture, a local version of what came to be known in the city as the "Vancouver Special": a cheaply built single-family dwelling that dominated the residential stock between the '50s and '80s. In Surrey, these sagging boxes, usually finished off with grimy stucco on top and rotting wood siding on the bottom, sometimes sported a shallow balcony on the semi-second floor — or, rather, a strip of metal fencing that was supposed to add adornment to the structure, but whose paint peeled, weeping rust stains down the house's stucco cheeks. Rot and rust: for me, these were the salient features of these neighbourhoods, which seemed always to be waterlogged by an unending season of precipitation — the sleety winter, the gusty storms of spring, the rainy Junes giving way to uncertain summers, the fog resolving into the ubiquitous droplets of Fall. Gentle weather, but damp.

I say "semi-second floor" because the first floor was semi-underground, making it a quasi-basement, really. These first floors, in the era I'm thinking of, either functioned as the "family room," with a pool table, a bar, and a fake-panelled back wall with a shelf for hockey and lacrosse trophies, or were converted to make an "in-law" suite for someone who was willing to pay "under the table" for this nearly under-the-ground accommodation.

But these houses down in Surrey were not, as I think of it now, Vancouver Specials after all, built as they were on slightly larger lots, and so shaped more like soggy loaves of Wonder bread than like the compact, two-storey structures that sprang up in the residential neighbourhoods north of the Fraser. These were Surrey's version of Lowry's "homeless homes with stoves full of old bones, and subaqueous basements, neglected and run down during the last years, houses once well situated, but now viewless as Shakespeare's winds, cackling, who knows, with poltergeists."

Perhaps the wretchedness I attach to these houses had more to do with the increasingly saturated nature of our own household, pickled as it was from the inside of my father's body outwards. If he was soused, then we were all wet around the edges, and the whole world was, as it seemed to me, one big sopping dishrag.

Mudflats

What would have constituted an escape for me? Surely not the more manicured city blocks we had left behind in the States, which were not really that well-kept in any case, sidewalks notwithstanding. No, I imagine for myself now the prospect of an alternative world that might have opened up had I somehow made a trip, in the summer of 1971, right up past Vancouver to the foot of those North Shore mountains we could see from the crest of the King George, where those squatters lived in their houses raised above the tidal waters. You wouldn't even care about the lack of sidewalks on the mudflats, since one shack was connected to the next by a network of quaint wooden boardwalks. If there had been no effort to establish a planned grid along which houses would be built, then there could be no imperfections where failure to maintain the grid occurred. These shacks just went up wherever they seemed to want

'Wooden boardwalks instead of concrete sidewalks.' Paul Spong's (left) and Helen Simpson's houses. Sean Malone

to take root, some back nearer the forest, on dry ground; some farther out on the tidal flats, raised up on their wooden posts; some right next to each other; some dotting the beach at a distance.

In a suburban neighbourhood, the gridded streets come first, along with the infrastructure; each house is then built on the lot accorded to it, in the most profitable manner for developers. But out on the flats the houses seemed merely to materialize of their own accord, some of them originally float houses, enlarged and embellished by what washed up at high tide; others small post-and-beam structures coming up from a scavenged platform on floats; one a "whorehouse" that had drifted over, or been towed (there were contradictory accounts), from elsewhere. To visit your neighbours you either walked across the grassy flats at low tide or, when the water was up, paddled a kayak or rowboat, or poled yourself astride a log. And then boardwalks on floats were built, the organic connecting tissue that turned the disparate dwellings into a settlement.

By 1971, two separate film teams arrived on the Maplewood Mudflats to document what must have been, by that time, a Vancouver "phenomenon" on the verge of disappearance. Chris Paterson and Robert Fresco came in from the NFB, and Sean Malone and Ed Dupuis from Seattle, and it seems that they were there at the same time, drawn as much, perhaps, by the very photogenic shacks as by the drama of the squatters' battle with the local mayor. Malone had originally intended to follow one of the squatters, whale researcher Paul Spong, up the coast to document his observation of orcas in the wild. But when he reached the North Shore and saw the squatters' village, he decided to go no farther: the mudflats would be the subject of his film.

The documentaries are different from one another: the NFB's *Mudflats Living* more journalistic in style; Malone's *Livin' on the Mud* lyrical, reflective. And yet it is almost as though the two teams had been set a challenge to see who could make the most melancholy movie with the following ingredients: no voice-of-God narration but only some meditative voices speaking over sunlit images; youthful laid-back longhairs contrasted with the ugly old mayor in his square suit; snippets of media coverage to tell the story of the squatters' battle with authorities; a group meal, the residents breaking bread together in harmony; folk music; showdown with bulldozers; and a conflagration for a conclusion.

Melancholy pervades, and what is the lost object of desire? The fantasy, so nurtured in the late '60s and '70s, that one could perch on the edge of the city and enjoy its cultural delights without being weighed down by the tedious need to contribute to its infrastructure? Or was it the dream of living with immediate access to nature (the estuarial setting, the mountains behind, the salt tides at one's door) without having to sacrifice the intellectual and social stimulation of the city? Maybe it was the fancy that it was still possible to practise self-sufficiency where your very habitation was concerned, because you could simply fabricate a shelter out of the odds and ends that came to hand, either from what the tides brought you, or from the houses that developers were destroying as they wastefully built their tall, sleek, high-rise structures.

Both films, even in their titles, emphasize the virtues of the mud, but the imagery they offer is uncharacteristic of the wet northwest climate that I remember, featuring as it does shot after shot of lightly clothed sunburned bodies frolicking among the tidal grasses, throwing Frisbees, jamming on banjos and drums, threading beads, gardening, washing, walking along the boardwalks, or just sitting under a cloudless sky as they speak to the camera. Only at the end is the constant sunshine contradicted by a kind of wintry coda. Blurry footage, as though borrowed from the news cameras of a December broadcast, shows a shack on fire against a darkening sky, squatters bundled against the cold, while fragments of disembodied dialogue are heard — the voice of Len George, a First Nations sympathizer from the nearby reserve: "They're going to look back over the land, the way it is now, after it's all built up, and they're going to say, why didn't we do something about it in 1970, or 1971, why didn't we fight for it then?" Or a woman who, earlier in the film, argued with bulldozer operators: "It's not just us, it's Nature that you're gonna wipe out here." Something was disappearing. But what exactly was it?

I learned that these films had been shown repeatedly to Vancouver audiences in successive decades, were still being shown in the twenty-first century, and that they accounted in large part for the survival of this squatters' community in the minds of Vancouverites who gave any thought at all to what distinguished their city from others. The Maplewood Mudflats squats had disappeared, but then, through these films and through journalistic references, or through tales passed down in the Vancouver art world, or in its world of architecture and design, or among its ecology promoters, or through photographs that would periodically show up in the *Vancouver Sun* or the *North Shore News*, or would be projected to audiences at tributes to the past — through all of these means, the afterimage of the shacks on the mudflats was retained on the city's collective retina to bolster Vancouver's sense of itself as a final frontier, even after its frontier days were long gone.

As a teenager, I was oblivious to the squatters up there on the distant North Shore mudflats. But having in recent years uncov-

'It's not just us, it's nature you're gonna wipe out here.'
Helen Simpson.
Courtesy Dan Clemens

ered those two documentaries about Vancouver's hippie past, I was immediately drawn into the world they evoked and wanted to know more. What was the story behind the images? What did it mean to want to live on the mud, to court a life of instability, of imminent eviction? "We couldn't own it," one of Lowry's squatting avatars says of his shack, "and if it ever got so we could, we wouldn't want it, it would be so different ... part of what's so wonderful there is that it isn't properly speaking anywhere at all, it's like living right out of the world altogether." To live "in the world," in other words, was to live in a house you could own; it meant being "permitted" to live by authorities with the power to grant you that permission, rather than just ... living. As though there could be a "pure" experience of living if you could only get "right out of the world."

Paul Spong, the original subject of Sean Malone's documentary, was easy to find, since he was one of the few residents to be named in the films and had acquired some fame in the interim as the activist who brought the Save the Whales cause to Greenpeace. To this day he lives on Hanson Island, on BC's Central Coast, so I talked to him on the phone rather than in person, though I still nurture the vague intention of making my way one day to OrcaLab, where he has set up his submerged microphones and cameras so that online whale-watchers from around the world can drop in to see the orcas he studies without disturbing them with the reverberations of a boat engine. Paul chatted with me but claimed not to have retained much in his memory after so many years. I should really, he urged, talk to his ex-wife, Linda, who had lived with him on the mudflats.

It wasn't until I talked with Linda at some length the following year that I realized she was one of the voices speaking in *Livin' on the Mud*, over her obscurely lit profile inside one of the shacks. A subtitle identifies her as Teusi, rather than Linda — a misspelling of her nickname, Tusi, I find out later. She's talking about hitchhiking and how she gets picked up by "other housewives." Housewife? How was it that this young dropout from the "Establishment," this apparently free-spirited woman living on the beach in this counter-cultural setting in 1971, thought of herself as a "housewife?" The other housewives are "curious," she says, and "after they talk to me for a while, I had two housewives coming down here looking for me. It was just an interesting, you know, experience to go with them, they are just very curious about the kind of people that live down here." She says she gets "sympathetic reactions from other people that have read about the mudflats, that I get picked up by. I've never really run into any hostile people."

I understood it now. It was as though "housewife" was a kind of mantra, repeated to ward off the hostility that could come her way, a woman hitchhiking back and forth from these mudflats that had a reputation already, since people were reading about them in the newspapers. But when the curious housewives met Tusi, they found she was just like them, another housewife. Or maybe it was that claiming a housewife identity was sort of like being in disguise, a masquerade of femininity, adopted to ward off criticism and condemnation from those who had agreed to conform to the customs of legitimate tenancy of one's marital abode.

Curbs and Dykes

But if she was a housewife, there was something about the mudflats that made living there more like playing house on the frontier, perhaps, than plodding through the classic housewife routine. I learned much from her as we talked in her Vancouver apartment in a downtown neighbourhood, neatly finished, these days, with cement curbs. When she had arrived in the city in the late '60s, she too noticed the absence of sidewalks, though for her, unlike for my teenage self, this was an exciting change from California. "I come from Los Angeles," she told me. "When I came to Vancouver I was thrilled, like, 'these streets don't even have curbs, we must be making homemade bread soon!'"

She was referring to the city itself, where she and Paul had first lived when they arrived in Canada. No curbs signified a more "Whole Earth" kind of lifestyle, where you opted out of store-bought food and went back to the basics: home-baked bread, granola, organic greens, and the like.

But the missing curbs were supplied at a rapid pace soon after Linda and Paul had come up from the States, as I discovered through another movie I stumbled upon while scanning the online Vancouver Archives, a sort of "orphan" film made by the city's engineering department in 1971. In this silent treasure, *Vancouver Low Cost Street Program*, inter-titles over a schematic map of the city report that as of 1962, Vancouver's residential streets were being "improved" at a glacial rate of only six blocks a year. The "bad conditions which prevailed" included high maintenance costs, ugly tattered side boulevards, and dusty residential areas. But a backward city could solve this unsightly problem by harnessing the power of an ingenious new contraption designed for "curb extrusion" —

that is, the pressing out of a perfect linear curb of wet concrete, as though squirted from a giant Play-Doh press.

The curb extruder garnered enthusiastic public response, the film tells us, and so the rate of improvement jumped to 250 blocks a year. Time-lapse photography shows block after block turning black on a map of the city as Vancouver's naked dirt is neatly sealed off with extruded concrete. No more mud, no more dust, no more unsightly streets! This has a marked psychological effect on the populace, so that soon we see the citizenry out trimming their shaggy hedges, mowing their overgrown lawns, and re-roofing their aging houses. Well-formed concrete truly does bring a ramshackle city into the modern age.

This little film, a gem from the time capsule I felt I was opening, spoke volumes to me and provided detail after detail about the era I had lived through. Not only did it treat me to an account of how the ditches I had so hated in my youth were being rapidly obliterated in the nearby city (Surrey did not seem to be enjoying any such "low cost street program" yet), but it was also very instructive in giving me a sense of where most Canadians, indeed most North Americans, were with regard to their understanding of how water works in its various cyclical patterns, vertical and horizontal. For this promotional film (I assumed it was produced as a model for spreading street improvement outward from the metropolis) expressed nary a thought about what the consequences would be if rainwater was diverted from areas of development, on a large scale, by impermeable avenues of concrete surfacing and drainage infrastructures. The film expressed the dream of a world in which water, earth, and even air remained always separate from each other: no opportunities for rain to collect in ditches and muddy the edges of the thoroughfare; no danger of dust arising from unpaved roads.

Vancouver's dream of an impermeable crust was untroubled by some alarming trends in its suburban lowlands to the southeast. Headline after headline in the Surrey weekly papers, from one year to the next, was preoccupied with the conundrum of failing dykes, seasonal flooding, and the question of who would pay for the damage done. The farmers on the flatlands along the Nicomekl and the Serpentine, for instance — two rivers that originated in the middle of the municipality and coursed their way southwest to the salt waters of Mud Bay — kept getting flooded out when the freshet from the snowmelt was bigger or combined with more precipitation than the usual frequent rainfall, or was deluged by the backwash from the salt tides that came farther up the rivers in a given season. Like the Fraser, the Nicomekl and Serpentine had originally been tidal estuarial rivers, the point where fresh water transitioned to salt water shifting from year to year depending on fluctuations in tide, snowmelt, and frequency of precipitation. But the entire Greater Vancouver area had been extensively dyked after major floods devastated most of the Fraser Valley in 1894 and 1948; indeed, you could say that by the mid-twentieth century, many of Vancouver's outlying suburban municipalities existed only by virtue of extensive dyking systems — Richmond, between the two major arms of the Fraser River, where the airport shared flatlands with huge agricultural swaths, was entirely surrounded by dykes. And so when the flooding kept happening on a local level in Surrey, it seemed to be a dyking issue, the only debate being who would pick up the repair bill: local, provincial, or federal government agencies?

An occasional article indicated that failing dykes were only a symptom of a larger, more systemic problem. In December 1973, for instance, in an item headlined "Heavy Rain Accentuates Deficiencies," the *Surrey–Delta Messenger* informed its readers that down on the "flat lands, water was unable to drain away quickly due to the fact that the ditches were already filled by runoff from melting snow, and high tides allowed the flood boxes to open for only a short time. When the water gradually began to recede it became evident that the ditches and culverts were too small to allow a quick runoff." This should have been no surprise, since earlier that year, in August, another article warned that "Dams won't solve flooding problems," and offered this quote from the dyking commissioner: "Dam reconstruction is necessary to prevent a major flood resulting from the breaking of the dams and the sea rushing in but it will do nothing to alleviate the problem caused by runoff from the highlands." The farmers, he added, "haven't been able to use the river water all summer because it was too salty."

Two problems were at the bottom of all this: first, the situation seemed to be one of the fundamental hazards of damming and dyking an estuarial area, where periodic tidal flooding had previously been the norm, in order to develop rich delta soil for farmland or, indeed, to convert it to residential use. But the problem was compounded by what was happening because of commercial, industrial, and residential development up on the neighbouring highlands.

As was becoming more and more clear to geographers and environmentalists, there had been enough loss of permeable surface area through extensive road and building construction in Surrey's townships of North Surrey, Newton, Guildford, that stormwater runoff was no longer being adequately absorbed in the areas where the rain fell — and it had to go somewhere. That somewhere was downstream, to the lowlands where the dykes and dams were eroding at a faster pace each year, in keeping with the rate of development upstream.

It was not until the last two decades that authorities have begun to experiment with a more comprehensive approach to what is now called, in the parlance of urban hydrology, storm water management. As a 2003 report by BC hydrologists put it,

> *When trees, vegetation and soils are replaced by roads and buildings, less rainfall infiltrates into the ground or is taken up by vegetation, which results in more rainfall becoming surface runoff. The key to protecting urban watershed health is to maintain the water balance as close to the natural condition as is achievable and feasible by preserving and/or restoring soils, vegetation and trees. But accomplishing this requires major changes in the way we approach urban drainage and in the way we develop land.*

Surrey, it would appear, was one of two BC locations (Simon Fraser University's UniverCity, on top of Burnaby Mountain, was the other) where this new approach was being investigated. Unsurprisingly, one of the main strategies was to undo, break up, and remove some of the hard concrete surfaces that had been established over the decades, so that rainwater, instead of being diverted through a system of streets, gutters, and extruded concrete curbs, could remain in the area where it had fallen and be absorbed back into the earth.

Apparently municipalities like Surrey learned the hard way that a "backward" trend in "street improvement" was the best way to go in areas like the Greater Vancouver region, where high precipitation converges with unpredictable snowmelts off the mountains and tidal surges from the ocean to make for volatile flood conditions. Now, on the City of Surrey website, you will find a page titled "Ditch Enclosures" that features a residential road with, yes, a grass-filled ditch running alongside it. "Ditches," the Surrey resident is informed,

> *play an important role in the overall drainage system of Surrey. Open ditches allow stormwater to infiltrate into the ground. This helps recharge groundwater and sustain creek base flows throughout the City. In rural areas, the City will not endorse ditch enclosures as roads with shoulders and more rural cross sections are better serviced through open systems.*

If you want to enclose your ditch, you must apply for a special permit. And even then, if you live in certain areas, like Bridgeview or on the "floodplain" (which is an extensive area) or within the Agricultural Land Reserve, Surrey is unlikely to grant you the privilege of enclosing your ditch. Curiously, however, Surrey's highlands do not seem to fall into the "restricted" category. Most of the ditches there have now been improved through the civilizing magic of the concrete extruding machine.

In Suspension

The mass-designed, mass-produced environments for an increasingly homogenized market of mass-consumers are no more than assemblies of material goods devoid of existential meaning ... The intense dialogue that takes place between squatters planning an invasion, and the administration are, with rare exceptions, totally lacking in the modern housing process.
— John Turner, 'THE SQUATTER SETTLEMENT: AN ARCHITECTURE THAT WORKS'

In the '70s, where there were ditches in Surrey or Vancouver, they were a sign that the civilizing process of urban development had not yet been completed. But the mudflats films presented a life voluntarily lived on the mud as a direct refusal to have any truck with concrete of any kind. You could say that concrete was the personified nemesis of mud. In the dreamy opening sequence of *Mudflats Living*, a soft-spoken male voiceover recites "Desiderata" — Max Ehrmann's poem ending with the image of the universe "unfolding as it should." We all had a copy of it on our bedroom walls in those days. As we are gently urged to "go placidly amid the noise and haste," birdsong punctuating the speaker's voice, the camera pans down from an early morning sun, rising behind a line of evergreens, to a back-lit Paul Spong, meditating, cross-legged, near the tomato plants on the deck of his wooden shack. With his gaunt face, long hair, and bushy beard he could be Prince Myshkin from Dostoevsky's *The Idiot*, or one of the Doukhobor Sons of Freedom, those exiles from Russia who settled in British Columbia, only to run naked through the streets in the early 1900s to assert their freedom from taxes and military service.

"Desiderata" continues as our view shifts to a young woman in an Indian-cotton skirt approaching a clear spring pool. She pauses (as though to weigh the pros and cons of being photographed), then pulls off her white T-shirt, baring her breasts as she scoops up water to bathe her face. "Be yourself," the voiceover seems to admonish her, to the accompaniment of the trickling stream, "especially do

'This cannot continue.' North Vancouver District Mayor Ron Andrews.
Mudflats Living

not feign affection, neither be critical about love." A dissolve takes us to a long shot of an elderly man in rubber boots walking along the flats at low tide, gulls and herons wheeling about, his form reflected upside down in a moss-bordered tidal pool; in the background, up against green foliage, the homely shacks are seen, while a cormorant ruffles its wings in the foreground. "With all its sham, drudgery and broken dreams, it is still a beautiful world."

But then the dream is abruptly broken by a sudden shock: the crying gulls are cut off by a grating voice insisting that "this cannot continue" — and we are confronted with the unpleasant image of a bloated face, slicked-back grey hair, a green plaid suit, tie, shirt. Across the bottom of the picture a label "switches on": Mayor Ron Andrews, his reddened face shiny in the fluorescent light of an institutional setting. Behind him, a green chalkboard, which doesn't seem to go at all with the summer-vacation imagery we've been feasting on. His voice is neither meditative nor poetic, but bureaucratic: "There's no building standards, there's very little power, and there's very poor water, and it just can't continue." He shakes his head.

Now, to contrast with the floating quality of the footage from the mudflats, a rapid montage sequence unfolds, at staccato speed, one shot after another: rectilinear city signage against ranks of highrises, cut across by power lines; a street light; a car tire; high-angle shot of a busy intersection; close-up of legions of feet scurrying over wet pavement; crowd of scowling faces under umbrellas; more traffic going; traffic coming; traffic sped up unnaturally fast; endless traffic crossing a bridge; and as the mayor's voice details the city's plans that are "firming up" — a "town centre" for the mudflats, to be anchored by a shopping centre, a theatre, marinas, and, vaguely, "all types of recreational, uh, artistic, etcetera, the whole gambit [sic]" — the montage images become obsessed with concrete, offering rapid-fire angles on high-rises, rigid towers, regularized ranks of cement cubicles, gray structure against a gray sky. The sequence ends with a close-up of wet cement gushing from a machine into a huge bucket, a digger dumping dirt, and a jackhammer breaking up asphalt, its drilling racket now accompanying the mayor's matter-of-fact drone.

Concrete extrusion as the epitome of The Establishment. Cement hardens into rigid, inhospitable forms, the message goes, whereas though mud may dry, it is reconstituted anew each day as the tides wash in and out, bringing new life for the birds to feed on, driftwood and flotsam to be gathered by human gleaners on the beach. This initial material opposition, between linearity, impermeability, and intractability on the one hand, and amorphousness, porosity, and flexibility on the other, filters further into a metaphorical realm as the film unfolds, until a theme of suspension emerges: as the earth and sand of the mudflats are always susceptible to a re-immersion in the ocean waters (and, in this estuarial setting, to a diffusion of sediment from the runoff that creeks bring down from the mountains), so too are other elements, material and immaterial, suspended, postponed, slackened. The aesthetic design of the shacks themselves — arguably the most memorable aspect of the squatters' community in Vancouver's collective consciousness — is premised on a principle of suspension. Most of them are built on pilings so that they hover above the always-shifting waters of the tidal flats, or on floats or log platforms so that they rise and fall with

Willie Wilson, collector. **Mudflats Living**

the water level. An ethic of accommodation to the fluctuating line between dry and wet prevails: no dams, no dykes, no culverts — no concrete intervention at all in the natural patterns of the mixing of water and earth at this liminal edge. By squatting here, the residents delay, if only temporarily, a concretization of the mayor's plans to replace this shifting periphery with a permanent "centre."

In this respect, the shacks also represent the suspension of an urban-defined progress, consisting as they do of a combination of driftwood (much of it fugitive detritus from BC's timber industry — logs that escaped the ubiquitous booms clotting the waterways, or cut lumber that detached itself from aging mills upstream, or even floating shacks that went adrift in a storm, meandered into the inlet, and ended up snagging in the area along the North Shore) and the demolition refuse from Vancouver's urban renewal schemes.

This was the era of fierce political battles in the city over whether whole neighbourhoods should be wiped out to make way for brutalist skyscrapers, mammoth shopping centres, and freeways; much of the Victorian and Edwardian housing stock was already coming down. They had been going on since Lowry's time, these city cleanup campaigns, wave upon wave: "the shingled houses were falling like ninepins, each day cupolas tumbled off the poor old steamboat Gothic buildings being torn down, like the trees, to make way for more soulless Behemoths in the shape of hideous new apartment buildings, yet more deathscapes of the future."

In *Mudflats Living* we meet Willie Wilson, who has made it his vocation to retrieve, little by little over time, the disparate elements of the demolished houses and bring them across the bridge onto the flats. He speaks to us from his perch among disused pipes and shutters, his dark gnarly hair reaching almost to his coveralls — "so stiff with oil" as Linda recalled — his black square glasses lending him a nerdy insouciance. "I don't know," he says, looking away, as though embarrassed by the wastefulness he's witnessed. "I just saw all this stuff ... being destroyed ... years ago. In Vancouver. And thought, well, I'll just pick out a few fine things and I might be able to use them for something and then I just noticed there was just ... one hell of a lot of it, being destroyed." The camera pans up a post to reveal the rusted frame of an old café chair silhouetted against the sky. All this stuff, he says, "either I could use it, or somebody else could. I built a house out of it, a castle, a rambling thing." And yes, some of the newel posts, bannisters, and gingerbread adornments he has collected compose structural or decorative elements in his rambling castle-shack, and those of his friends. But most of his gleanings remain liberated from their original function, heaped in piles of like objects, as though they have returned to an open-air warehouse of sorts. Or they become the elements of artistic expression, the art of found objects: one resident speaks to us from behind a gently swaying grid of nails hung by fishing line from a platform overhead — his latest creation; or we catch a glimpse, on a kitchen wall, of a mismatched checkerboard of wooden squares, each with a circle inside — these are corner blocks, removed from their "proper" positions at the four angles of a Victorian window frame and regrouped into this "useless" adornment; or a medley of empty bottles dangle near a window, sunlight refracting through the glass. The artist with the nail installations says he mainly makes objects himself, "an artistic piece," whereas you take someone like Willie "and he, uh, he collects his stuff." As though to say that they are both to be considered artists. They just have somewhat different relations to their materials.

It is an aesthetic of suspension in more than one way — suspended objects signifying the suspension of "use-value" in general, an ethic of purposelessness. Willie the Collector, his neighbours call him, an artist who by design or by compulsion lives out the precepts of Walter Benjamin's "collector," making the "glorification of things his concern." To him, Benjamin wrote,

> fell the task of Sisyphus which consisted of stripping things of their commodity character by means of his possession of them. But he conferred upon them only a fancier's value rather than use-value. The collector dreamed that he was in a world which was not only far-off in distance and time, but which was also a better one, in which to be sure people were just as poorly provided with what they needed as in the world of everyday, but in which things were free from the bondage of being useful.

'A rambling thing' — Willie Wilson's house, with Tom Burrows's sculptures in the foreground.

David Wisdom

It is partly the presence of this collector of the city's cast offs, then, that marks the mudflats as Vancouver's dreamed-of better world, both close and far-off: close in distance; far off, now, in time.

Even language begins to lose its use-value on the mudflats. During a meal sequence, the camera hovers near a toddler holding an orange up to his mouth. "Justin," a girl's voice says, "you can't eat an orange. Here, you can eat an apple," and a hand switches the fruit as the child tries to copy the girl's voice, "ba-ba." Then the girl chimes in, mimicking the meaningless sound, "ba-ba-ba," and we cut to a close-up of a dangling chandelier crystal, freed from its fellows on a one-time ornate light fixture, a cobweb clinging to its edge as though to emphasize how long it has been in "disuse."

In the other film, *Livin' on the Mud*, this linguistic oblivion is intensified when we are introduced to Tom Burrows, an artist in a French beret, who takes a minute from raking his pile of stones to muse on the practice of his art in the mudflats setting. When he came back to Vancouver after having been in London on a fellowship, he says, he was wandering around, "walked over this way, suddenly I found this cabin ... was the absolute answer to all my desires." As the camera focuses in on his face, framed by straggly

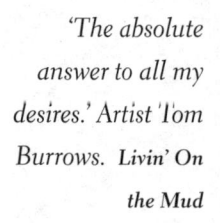

'The absolute answer to all my desires.' Artist Tom Burrows. **Livin' On the Mud**

Dutch-boy locks, his speech becomes less intelligible — murmurs, hesitantly, his lips barely moving, and we hear tentative snatches of thought:

> *want you to make an object, for me, . . . and you can come and see it, take pictures of it, . . . no no this is a hypothetical situation, then I think, uh, how much money, I think, uh, how much will I sell my soul for 'cause it's not a public thing, I'm making this thing for . . . that don't really agree too much with it anyway, is it worth ten thousand is it worth twenty thousand? Or maybe I shouldn't do it at all.*

Articulation itself is a dubious prospect, it seems, apt to lead to some sort of commercial transaction that will negate the very basis of art, of life. The camera pans across Burrows's installation: scavenged metal hoops, bars, rope, chains, driftwood, all of it arranged on or plunged into the mud. When the tide comes in, loops and angled lines meet their reflections on the glassy surface — only the periodic rise of placid water can complete the geometrical forms the found elements trace out. Circles, triangles, chains seem suspended, floating oddly, because of the indistinction between water and air. Malevich come to rest on the Canadian mudflats, occupying as much a temporal as a spatial zone.

Working on Oneself

> *The squatter barriada-builder who chooses to invest his life's savings in an environment that he creates, forms himself in the process. The person, as the member of a family and of a local community, finds in the responsibilities and activities of home-building and local improvement the creative dialogue essential for self-discovery and growth.*
> — John Turner, 'THE SQUATTER SETTLEMENT: AN ARCHITECTURE THAT WORKS'

> *I could feel the improvement. Little by little self-discipline, a sense of humor and our happy life together were wreaking a miracle. Was this effort toward life and health merely to be a probationship for death?*
> — Malcolm Lowry, 'THE FOREST PATH TO THE SPRING'

Linda doesn't appear much in the films, so her perspective on the mudflats came to me through my conversations with her, as reminiscences. Not so where Paul Spong was concerned. Although the filmmakers call on many of the squatters to contribute their observations, their cameras return most insistently to this Zen-softened mad scientist, drawing from him gentle ripostes to the mayor's harrumphs, an impassioned exchange with sheepish workers sent to demolish the cabins, and a mild lesson shared with Yashi, his toddler son. At one point he begins to recount his life story: he was born and educated in New Zealand, he says, having spent an idyllic childhood by the ocean there. He came to California to study physiological psychology with the famous psychologist Donald Lindsley at UCLA, where he earned his PhD in 1966. Then, around the same time my grandparents were setting up in the motel business, he was offered a "unique trip" that brought him with Linda up across the border to Vancouver, to work in neurophysiology at UBC while studying the behaviour of the first killer whale to be held in captivity, at the Vancouver Aquarium. "I came to Vancouver at that time," he reflects, "a fairly highly motivated scientist, I would think." The camera cuts to another flats dweller at this point, and by the time it returns to Paul he is describing the "headspace" he was in when he arrived at the flats as "terribly scattered ... my head was just literally shattered by experiences that I had had, in the previous year." What had happened, then, between his employment at the aquarium and his arrival on the mudflats in a shattered state?

In 1972, Vancouver audiences of the film — and perhaps Canadians in general — would have been able to fill in the blank, at least partly, having caught, no doubt, the media coverage of a shocking announcement Spong made about his findings at the aquarium. The whales, he asserted, had become depressed in captivity. They were suffering from sensory deprivation and, his most outlandish claim according to aquarium officials, they were communicating their suffering to him. He urged the aquarium to set them free. Not too long after, Spong himself was set free, fired from his position at the aquarium. What the public perhaps did not know was that he was also persuaded by the head of the psychiatry unit where he had been working as a researcher to become a patient in the university

'My head was just literally shattered.' Paul and Yashi Spong. **Mudflats Living**

hospital's psychiatric ward.

Neither film broaches this story of Paul's pleas on behalf of the whales, nor the subsequent disciplinary treatment he received — maybe because whale activism had barely reached public consciousness by 1971 (this was something Paul later brought to the emerging Greenpeace movement), or maybe because it would open a whole new kettle of fish, so to speak, and distract from the films' central focus on mudflats existence.

Wanting to find out more about Paul's time at the aquarium, I turned to Rex Weyler's substantial tome on the history of Greenpeace, which presented Paul as a victim of psychiatric suppression, his political stance on the whales undermined by the impression, given out by his superiors, that he had mental problems and should not be taken seriously. After all, the aquarium had a lot at stake, having paid a hefty $25,000 for the whale Paul wanted to liberate.

Linda's account was more nuanced, suggesting there was a side to Paul this tale of political suppression was not capturing. As though wanting to understand the personal positions of all involved, she tried to see the situation from the point of view of the university and aquarium officials, who were dealing with this researcher who did not "wear a white shirt or tie or anything," whose hair was "huge, the way he looked!" They had been gracious, she thought, to "keep him around ... let him go as far as he did."

> And the final thing was, because Paul was doing an experiment with crystal glass, you know, rubbing the rim of it, to make the sound and see if the whale liked it, and the glass fell in the pool, and they really thought this was a danger to the whales. So that's why he was fired. I mean it was that kind of thing.

But Linda's husband, Bill, here interjected with a defense of Paul, saying that this was merely a "technicality, we got something here, we got a reason to get rid of him!"

"Yeah," Linda agreed, though perhaps still with some doubt, "they wanted to get rid of him, and they got rid of him."

But Linda seemed to be saying that the emotional distress Paul had fallen into during his research with the whales — as though he had begun to identify with them, in their captivity — was not to be denied. On the one hand, it seemed that something had to be done for Paul. But on the other, the psychiatric facilities themselves seemed to be exacerbating the problem. Paul's office was upstairs, she recalled,

> so they just sent him down to the nuthouse (we called it the nuthouse), and, well, anyway, at the time, it was pretty wild, because, you know, they gave him all these drugs, but they didn't seem to calm him down at all ... he was so manic, and we had just read One Flew Over the Cuckoo's Nest the prior November, so he was organizing, there was Big Nurse, and he was organizing the patients, and he'd bring them all out to this place that we lived in at West Third Avenue, on day trips, and I had, like, I had this little baby ... and there would be all these patients from the clinic ... and they were all so drugged that they were the sweetest, most wonderful people. I don't know if they always were like that, but they were so mellow to talk to, and then they'd all go back.

As Paul's efforts at liberation shifted from the whales to his fellow patients in the psych ward, this Ken Kesey drama was apparently more than Linda had bargained for, especially given that she was now grappling with the care of a newborn. It would have been hard to blame Paul, apparently: "He was so charismatic that even in his delusional craziness he could get a following from the outside. It was just amazing." Finally, she said, "UBC put him under sleep therapy. They put him asleep for a week, I think ... He needed that, he really needed it, to clean his system out, of everything."

When he awakened from his curative slumber, she concluded, Paul felt "really bad about it. He said, you know, I've really blown it." As for Linda, she had gotten to the point where she was "pretty burnt out ... having a baby and all this stuff," and she thought, "I can leave Paul." She went away for three or four months, stayed with a friend, and by the time she came back, Paul had moved onto the mudflats, where she joined him for the next two years.

So this was the backstory to Paul's account of himself to the filmmakers, that his head had been shattered. "The mudflats is unquestionably, well you can't live around here without your head being cooled out," he says. Then, over a floating, wavering shot from out on the water, a twisted knot of driftwood sliding by to reveal one of the shacks up on the shore, the sun glinting off the many-paned windows cobbled together on its southern exposure: "The tides flow in and out," Paul murmurs, "and you begin to adjust your natural biological rhythms to the rhythms that are already existing in nature, I think. And this has a tremendously liberating effect on a person. I find the mudflats very conducive to working on oneself."

If he could not succeed in freeing the whales, at least not yet, might he free himself? Might this be the locale to practise one's liberation, a project that would extend even to the next generation? For it was not only his own headspace that was in question, but that of his child as well, little Yashi, the infant that Linda had brought with her when she moved in with Paul. In the films there seem to be kids all over the place, carefree toddlers running along the wooden walkways, dipping into a barrel of soup, paddling astride a piece of driftwood. "People tell us this is a terrible environment, a terrible way to be living," Paul says. "It's so meagre, the existence here is so meagre. But that's not the point. The point is what kind of environment do you provide for the heads that are functioning there?" We back slowly away from a spider in the centre of its web, the suspended bottles adorning a cabin coming into view.

> *And I particularly am looking at my child, and I think that the kind of life that my child is exposed to at the mudflats is the healthiest thing that a child can possibly be exposed to. He has complete freedom of movement [here we see a bare-bottomed toddler in a pullover sweater, a baby-bottle dangling from his clenched teeth to leave his hands free for balance as he scampers along one of the boardwalks], he can run around wherever he likes. I don't have to bother about whether or not he's going to be running up on the highway and getting hurt. I don't have to be afraid, he doesn't have to be afraid, he learns to get around without fear. And that's a very basic thing we have to learn. Mudflat living for people, I think, is completely healthy, and I'm talking about mental health, right? I'm a psychologist; I'm primarily a student of behaviour, and as a student of behaviour looking at the kind of life that goes on outside, and comparing the total plasticity, total denial, really, of reality, I think. And comparing that kind of life with the kind of life that children are being exposed to on the mudflats ... We're raising a generation now of children who are healthy, and they're going to be healthy bodies, and they're going to be healthy heads; and around the mudflats you get both things happening.*

The message is a familiar one — life in a natural setting, away from the dangers of civilization (like the cars and logging trucks barrelling along the King George Highway, just a few yards away from the front door of our A-frame at the motel), is going to be better for the growing child, body and mind. And what makes the environment so beneficial? The absence of timidity in relation to mobility — the child develops a fearlessness, confidence, a self-reliant attitude about the world around him, and doesn't even, it appears, need any parental supervision. Because the parents, too, need not be "bothered," need not be tormented by the burden of responsibility for this little life, flourishing in the mud with all the other life. People may think it's a meagre place to live, but the mudflats signify, above all else, abundance of life.

There is another aspect to this idea of abundance out of meagreness; it has to do with being beholden to no one, choreographing a life apart from the forced march of a nine-to-five job or its counterpart, the slow grovel of the unemployed schmuck on assistance.

'He has complete freedom of movement.'
Toddler on the mudflats. **Mudflats Living**

In the documentaries we find what seems to be an unattached woman. She's the one whose graceful fingers, in close-up, pick out a bead and add it to a necklace she's stringing as she shares the story of her previous life in the Establishment world. Sun-browned legs, auburn hair blowing in the summer breeze, she tells us about "working for the telephone company," her North Van accent seeming to me the epitome of how Canadians spoke in those days. She was "an assistant senior payroll clerk class two group seven," she recites, just the slightest note of sarcasm conveying what she thinks of the kind of bureaucratic job she had for sixteen years, contributing to unemployment insurance and welfare, then collecting on it for a year after that. "I know what it's like when, thinking of myself paying taxes, and someone else living on those taxes for nothing. It's a drag," she says. But now she doesn't depend on the state. "The satisfaction of just surviving; having to survive without welfare, and doing it on my own ... it's much more of a dance than ever I was able to do." The dance of doing it on one's own. The film implies that somehow she stays afloat doing this dance of survival, and it is primarily the squatters' rent-free condition that provides the buoyancy for that dance.

Drop-In

The idea of dropping out to "work on oneself" or to perform the "dance of survival" was not a popular one south of the Fraser in Surrey. Here, when the idea of "work" came up, it had to do with whether one could find it or not; whether one was actively engaged in gainful employ or mooching off the municipality's welfare ticket. Welfare was a municipal affair in the early '70s, administered by mayors and local councils. One summer, 349 people on Surrey's public assistance roll received letters telling them their benefits would be cut off because council had "approved a recommendation from the Welfare Committee that the unemployed employables on Welfare would be asked to seek work in the berry fields rather than accept welfare cheques." Mayor Bill Vander Zalm announced that the policy would remain in effect until "no more work" was available. The same thing was going on in neighbouring municipalities as well, though in the case of Burnaby, "employable" persons were at least referred to the municipal personnel office for screening and classification for jobs inside or outside the municipality.

Surrey's mayor must have been taken to task for this early instance of his intolerance for apparent laggards, because the same article reports that one alderman in Surrey suggested they should perhaps follow Burnaby's example and find a better plan for "employables." "We might save face by coming up with some constructive suggestions rather than the one to pick berries." Someone at the newspaper had a sense of humour. Next to one of the stories about Vander Zalm's hardline policy on welfare was an ad from a business just up the King George from us, Roath's Pawn Shop: "Cash Short? Borrow ours!" it says over a cartoon of a man receiving a bag of money.

It was in this atmosphere, where disdain for "unemployed

employables" combined with a fear of what would happen if the local youth decided, en masse, to "drop out," that a novel scheme emerged in our own municipality of Surrey: to foster opportunities for young people to "drop in" via community-sponsored drop-in centres — a new idea in this part of the world that had organized itself around church activities, closed fraternal clubs, hockey, lacrosse, baseball, and the Legion marching band.

My own diary of the time takes its place now among the weekly papers, the documentary films, and the minutes of council meetings as part of the archives I'm raiding here. During my second year of junior high at West Whalley, a persuasive young man named Steve appeared one day in our guidance class at school. Steve had come from a nearby crisis centre and was looking for "volunteers, to work at a new drop-in place at an elementary school, on the flats," I reported. By "the flats" I meant Bridgeview, that small neighbourhood I mentioned at the beginning of this book, nestled in with the railyards, lumber mills, and other industrial concerns just downhill from us, where the King George Highway levelled off at the Fraser River's edge. I have already described how Surrey served as a sort of "whipping boy" for Vancouver — shoring up the big city's sense of its superiority. If abuse breeds abusers, then Surrey, in turn, directed its scorn at the most wretched of its downtrodden districts: the riverside community of Bridgeview. Thus, in the early 1970s, Bridgeview was known to me for two things: as the sketchy neighbourhood that our maid walked up from each day to help us clean motel units for an undoubtedly paltry wage; and as what my "upper-middle-class" peers (as I called them in my diary), who lived in the only slightly more well-heeled suburban tracts surrounding our school, called "Ratsville" to express their disdain for the deplorable sanitary conditions to be found "down there." It wasn't a railroad track that divided the poor from the middlebrow in our district, but something like a sense of elevation: if you lived "on the flats," you inhabited a distinctly different world than if you lived "on the hill."

Need I add that my own status, as a dweller on a commercial lot where the highway began its descent to the "flats," was suspect?

Maybe it was this fragility about my social status that contributed to my decision to see what I could offer to the less fortunate. I'm sure I did not consciously realize this, but it is possible that by engaging in a philanthropic endeavour I was asserting my superiority over those who were to receive its benefits.

A few days later my friend Sharron and I rode our bikes down to Bridgeview and joined about twelve other teenagers for a meeting at the elementary school library. The goal of the project was never entirely clear to me, though I gathered it was intended "to give people with nothing to do, something to do," and involved being trained to better communicate with people, communication being a key catchword of the era. To accomplish this, we were to engage in exercises, like volleyball and crab soccer (where you scuttle about the gym floor in the crab position: hands and feet on the ground, stomach toward the ceiling), that were designed to make us more aware of our "bodies, minds, and surroundings," so that when the drop-in centre opened we could be "sort of super friends to anyone who wants to drop in." If I was uncertain who those people with "nothing to do" might be, it could have been because the drop-in was "still in its experimental stage and we, the staff, are guinea pigs," though, as I added optimistically, I preferred to think of us as "Pioneers!"

That the citizens of Bridgeview had other ideas about where to find "something to do" was not so subtly hinted at when Sharron and I came out of the meeting to find that someone had let the air out of our bicycle tires. I don't know if I truly did not read this prank as conveying a message, or if I simply was unwilling to admit that our services might not be welcomed by Bridgeview's youth. I made no comment except to remark that we had to walk to the nearest gas station before we could ride back up the hill.

I did not know it then, but some browsing in the local papers from those years tells me that the idea of the Bridgeview drop-in centre had been brewing for some time. The latest chapter in an effort to bring much-needed social services to the youth of our growing municipality, this centre was sponsored by an organization called Inter-section, founded in 1970, just as we were arriving in Canada, by maverick psychologist Andrew Feldmar, who was working at the Surrey health clinic at the time, an agency that was "hard-pressed to keep pace with the number of referrals being received." Article after article from that year showed Feldmar and others meeting with the Parks and Recreation Commission, the Y, the Kinsmen, making their case for at least a trailer where "kids could come and talk to each other, play a few games, or just have a change of scenery." There was a need, Feldmar believed, "for some 'less conventional' approaches to the question of young people and their leisure time." By "less conventional," Feldmar was referring to activities that did not involve a stick, a puck, or a baseball bat, and even ventured so far as to suggest that "not everyone likes sports."

The idea that a space should be provided for kids to "hang out" was not a popular one, and many objected that it would attract hippies and druggies. "People are afraid to pay money for a place where kids might sit and do nothing," Feldmar commented. "I guess they don't place any value on personal growth and that sort of thing." It was as though Feldmar wanted to bring to Surrey just a smidgeon of what the Maplewood squatters were enjoying up on their mudflats — space and time to "sit and do nothing," to engage in the kind of idleness that might lead to "personal growth." Or to work, perhaps, if not at a job, then on oneself.

I don't think anyone in Surrey knew then just how radical Feldmar's own background was. This didn't come out until decades later, when he made news in 2007 because of an incident at the border — no doubt the same Peace Arch crossing where my family had entered the country. He was making a routine trip from his Vancouver home to meet a friend in Seattle when customs officials Googled his name and came up with an academic paper he had published in 2001, reporting on scientific experiments in the '60s involving hallucinogenic drugs as a form of therapy. Because he himself had taken LSD as part of his research at the time (just a few years before his appearance in Surrey), he was denied entry to the United States under Homeland Security regulations and banned

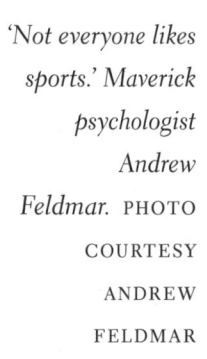

'Not everyone likes sports.' Maverick psychologist Andrew Feldmar. PHOTO COURTESY ANDREW FELDMAR

from ever entering the country again. Never mind that Feldmar was internationally respected for his efforts to treat drug addiction and PTSD. His persona non grata status persists to this day. The ordeal was ludicrous enough to merit a "Nailed 'Em" episode on the Colbert Report.

So Feldmar's own stance on "drugs" was, to say the least, a complicated one compared to that of the average citizen of Surrey. During meetings discussing whether the drop-in project was to be given a green light, Inter-section was bombarded with questions: Might the program encourage rather than hinder unwanted youth culture elements in the suburban community? Was it going to give advice to teenage girls when "such matters" were best handled by responsible parents? Would it offer an alternative to what one questioner thought was the "'shrug-off' approach by some teachers to the use of drugs?" If the drop-in centre didn't take a determined anti-drug stand, "there's no knowing where it will all end."

But "drugs," Inter-section replied, "are a symptom of deeper complex problems. The problems must be tackled first. Persons with an alcohol, smoking, soft or hard drug problem cannot be approached with a 'bang on the head' technique. He must be listened to by someone in whom he has trust."

Coincidentally, the president of the Alcoholism Foundation of BC was quoted in a June 1971 issue of the *Surrey–Delta Messenger* saying that despite best efforts to treat it, alcohol addiction was growing at such a rapid pace in the province that the social damages were alarming. The same article quoted the report of Canada's Le Dain Commission of Inquiry into the Non-Medical Use of Drugs, which had established not only that alcoholism was "still Canada's number one drug problem," but that alcohol abuse in British Columbia was "above the national average." I could attest, from my own experience, that it was much more endemic among our parents' generation than among the teenagers. Consider the remark in a *Surrey Leader* article in the Fall of 1971: in "Board Inspects Teen Dances," two Parks and Rec commissioners reported on a surprise visit they had made to a teen dance, where they were assaulted not only by the "smell of pot in the air," but also by the band's music, which seemed comparable to "the noise of a papermaking machine in a paper mill." But while a few of the teens were "under the influence of liquor," one commissioner admitted that "with 475 teenagers at this dance, there were less the worse for wear because of liquor than at the banquet and dance involving 170 adults held the following week."

In any case, the primary goal of Inter-section was not to wipe out drug use, but to begin to build an infrastructure of activity that included something other than sports — the idea being that a greater diversity of opportunities for self-development would have a side effect of mitigating substance abuse.

By hook or by crook, Feldmar and his associates managed to secure a cast-off bus and some basic funds from volunteer organizations, and by January 1971 the first Inter-section drop-in was born — not in Bridgeview yet, but in Unwin Park, about six miles south of our motel. It had a rocky start and attracted criticism when a psychedelic "paint-in" to decorate the bus (on a particularly rainy day) resulted in a "ruddy mess," according to one indignant alderwoman. But Feldmar was optimistic, emphasizing the drop-in's mission to "put the kids in touch with people who can help them with their special interests, whether it be making a movie or whatever." Skeptics may have doubted the need for or efficacy of this hangout for youth, but by the end of that year it was reported that over 1,300 calls had been handled on the "crisis phone lines" in December alone, and the centre had increased its service from eighteen to a hundred hours per week.

That summer, Bridgeview residents approached the Surrey school board about increasing facilities for young people in their isolated neighbourhood, calling for their own drop-in centre and a swimming pool. The school board would only go so far as to loan out the elementary school for a drop-in centre, provided that money could "be found elsewhere to pay for proper supervision." Inter-section must have stepped up to the plate with some rudimentary funding and manpower — or, rather, teenpower — since by the Fall of 1972 my fellow classmates and I were being trained to be "super friends" to the disadvantaged youth down on the flats.

But there was a bigger issue at stake. The municipality refused to invest in a swimming pool (though it was building new pools in every other Surrey neighbourhood) because "the future of Bridgeview is up in the air at the present time. Surrey Council is debating whether it should remain a residential area or whether it should become industrial."

Family

> The others ... were all, with one exception, deep-sea fishermen who had been here many many years before the summer people came, and who had their houses here by some kind of "foreshore rights" allowed to fishermen. The exception was the Manx boatbuilder ... he seemed to be the father or grandfather of most of the other fishermen, so that, in the way of Celts, it was a little like a big family.
> — Malcolm Lowry, 'THE FOREST PATH TO THE SPRING'

The films, the news coverage, and some of the recollections of the mudflats squatters I interviewed suggested that part of the "freedom" for heads and bodies that Paul Spong championed in the North Shore Maplewood setting had to do with experimentations in "family" life. The mudflats was where one hoped for a fresh perspective on the very convention of family; a new kind of family could be brought to life, shaped and freed by a relaxing of architectural structures, by the way one family was physically situated in relation to another, and, indeed, by the definition of what counted as "family" in the first place.

The NFB was tentatively exploring alternative family arrangements in other films of this period. In Kathleen Shannon's short 1974 doc titled *Extensions of the Family*, for example, a group of thirteen adults and children live under the same roof in a large Vancouver house, sharing the domestic responsibilities of cooking, cleaning, and childcare, with the mortgage on the house distributed among four of the residents. This was the urban version of rural communal situations that had sprung up all over North America and elsewhere, a "continuing experiment with 'alternatives' to the prevailing nuclear family structure" according to the film's study guide. I don't know when and where this surprisingly countercultural vehicle was shown; part of the "Working Mothers" Series headed up by Shannon, it may have been included in screenings for groups of women across Canada who were just beginning to explore their options in a world they hoped to change. The study guide was provocative in its needling of conventional family arrangements: "Who benefits from living in a nuclear family?" it asked. "Can government define what is good for our children? Who should decide? Is it easier to share household responsibilities in a large 'chosen' family than in a nuclear family?" But then again, as though to be balanced, "What problems would this 'solution' create for you?"

I wondered if these were the same kinds of alternative communal family arrangements to be found on the mudflats. Watching *Mudflats Living*, I was struck by one intrepid young woman in pigtails who didn't seem to be much older than I was in 1971. Her youthful face with its upturned nose and rounded cheeks appears barely more mature than the face of the infant she totes on her hip while tending a vegetable patch up near the forested area between the shoreline and the Dollarton Highway. Child mother? Unnamed, she contrasts her current living environment with the one she knew from a more conventional past life: "When I was in Ottawa," she says,

> *I lived in the city, or I live in the city when I live in Ottawa, and it's just like house to house, streets and roads and cement and no backyard ... Out here ... you are living by yourself but yet with a lot of other people. Where everybody's together ... Whereas living in the city, you're living beside someone who you don't really know. There's no communication between you and your neighbour ... Whereas out here, you're living beside someone, and you know that person, and you're a part of that person just like that person's a part of you, but yet you're still on your own and that person is on their own. But you know that if you need them, that they're there.*

She's the quintessential transplant from "back East" — moving from Canada's bureaucratic capital to its West Coast frontier and defining that difference as a move from the stifling urban to the liberating rural. But whose life is she a part of on the mudflats, aside from the life of that infant she is looking after? Is that her again in the scenes of the communal meal, cracking eggs into a frying pan sizzling with bacon? Or scrubbing laundry down by the spring? Unlike Linda, in her brief appearance as Tusi — the mother in the Spong family trio — she makes no reference to her "family" status whatsoever, as though the connectedness to one's neighbours surpasses or counteracts one's role in a domestic familial structure. No "cement" keeps you hemmed in with the monadic family unit. Instead, you communicate freely with others regardless of their "relation" to you: they are a part of you and you of them, even as you can be "on your own" as well. Does this strike me as the rote recital of a recently conned bit of rhetoric only because of the demise of such experiments in the intervening years? Or does the film's visual evidence suggest that things had not, after all, changed very much for women, even in this new life among the other mudflats dwellers? In scene after scene, women are depicted performing the same tasks that consumed my own mother, and which were in store for me as well, should I take a certain path in life: the cooking and serving of meals, the washing of clothes, the bathing, the feeding, the monotonous tending of infants. Maternal idealization in the mudflats idyll. Unlike Tusi, Pigtails doesn't tell us she is a housewife — makes no mention of her infant at all, as though the question of her better life as a mom speaks for itself.

So what could be found as alternative family on the mudflats? A communal camaraderie that had broken free from the doomed routines with one's blood relatives? The films imply an idealized shared communal life that apparently was not the case, according to Linda. Sure, "we were sort of living in proximity with each other, but not too close ... we weren't really like a big commune." Because of their dispersion out across the beach, they were probably farther from their neighbours than the people living in houses in the Surrey suburbs, where fences and hedges were erected to ensure privacy. So was their way of living a challenge to conventions of bourgeois suburban family life? "It wasn't like we were fighting middle-class values," Linda recalled. "It's just that, here was a really unique place to live, and, well, we bought our house, and Paul was still at UBC. He was, you know, 'Dr. Paul Spong,' and he'd go there and do his work with the meditators, and so he had a job, he'd go every day, and I was a stay-at-home mom, with my little boy, and my house had the same feeling that [my current house] has." They were, she believed, "opportunists, young opportunists who happened to find this very groovy, unusual place to live."

It was "just a moment in time," Linda recalled, for these people who had not necessarily known each other before, and who went on to live variously conventional lives afterward: the son of their neighbour Tom Burrows "grew up to be a 'middle-class man,'" for instance; Willie Wilson's daughter "went to university," and her mother "ended up working for BC Ferries." It was a moment in time.

But there was something about that moment that did depart from the moments Linda said she lived subsequently, and today. "We had all read the book by Ram Dass, *Be Here Now*. We were sort of 'here now,' we didn't really have plans for the future, or we hadn't thought about making plans for the future. We were quite young ... I think I was twenty-two, twenty-three at the time." And, indeed, her recollections were sprinkled through with references to the Ram Dass imperative. I asked if, after their eviction from the mudflats, she had followed the subsequent events in the area. "No," she said, "we were so busy living, we were 'here now,' we ... it's only now that we aren't 'here now' anymore."

Being "here now" meant not looking forward, not looking back; for Linda it meant a kind of oblivious disconnect from one's own family of origin. Her mother, she said, had moved at a young age from Chicago to California to become an actress, married a teamster, and although she had five children in seven years, she was no stay-at-home mom. "She actually ended up teaching," Linda said, though "she was in a few plays. She was this total eccentric, but I didn't know that she was that eccentric until I left home." She described her family as "not very close," and as though to illustrate what she meant by this, she told me about what she called a "naïve" notion she had: "I really thought that people flew away from home like birds. I don't know why I thought that, but somehow that was in my mind ... we didn't really have much contact with relatives."

Living "here now" meant, among other things, that it would not occur to one to return to the nest for a visit with mama bird. When a guest announced that he was going to visit his own mother, for instance, Linda was surprised. "You're kidding!" she gasped. "You still visit your mother?" It wasn't until he pointed out that Linda might want Yasha to visit her someday that she could conceive, for the first time, the convention that adult children might periodically return to see their parents. Being "here now" meant not imagining for herself a future in which she might be visited by her grown-up son.

But what were the other groupings of people on the mudflats? Was the settlement merely a replica, after all, of suburban nuclear families living in proximity with each other, distinguished only by the severing of their ties with a previous generation, striving to live in the present moment? It was implied, in some of the conversations I had, that loose-knit groups of people who lived, but more importantly worked, together on the flats called themselves "family," but always in contrast to the kind of nuclear family to be found in the residential neighbourhoods of municipalities like Surrey.

"There were all these family names," recalled artist and carpenter Ian Ridgway. "There was the Out to Lunch Bunch and the Loony Tooners and the Banana Brothers, and we wanted something like that too, that we could really shelter behind so we didn't have to say, No, this is the guy that's running things." By "we" he meant he and Dan Clemens and his fellow artisans, and the "family name" was a way to counter the kind of hierarchy that characterized the corporate-style businesses you'd find in The Establishment.

Together, Ian and Dan had been building fanciful booths for rock festivals and for Pleasure Faires, versions of which were popping up all over North America, featuring craft stands where you could buy leather goods, jewellery, silk-screened T-shirts, and the like. The BC Pleasure Faires, held in the Fraser Valley or on the North Shore during the period of the squatters' village, were attended by a generation of youth looking for a more relaxed, even clothing-optional, atmosphere than what they would find across the inlet at the more traditional Pacific National Exhibition. The Pleasure Faires had the same countercultural vibe as rock concerts, except that, as squatter Roger Brewton put it, at the rock concerts

> *you are all going there to look at somebody perform, and get high, so it's a direct audience and performer thing, whereas with the faire, everyone was a performer, and everyone was the audience ... everyone would come and see us with our long hair, [and] we were fascinated with everyone who came to see us ... just an interchange of culture, when people would come and realize that we were not scary. [They wouldn't get] such an attitude because maybe we're not doing anything so weird.*

People would stay for a few days at a time, camping out, cooking over open fires, or waiting in line at the corn-on-the-cob stand — loose aggregations of people affiliated by shared countercultural values more than by conventional family ties.

Ian and Dan were building their first booth in 1970, Ian recalled, at the Strawberry Mountain Rock Festival, out beyond Mission up the Fraser Valley:

> *It was all made out of this wonderful gingerbread, and at that same time, Willie Wilson pulls out of his truck this big curtain. It's an old cinema curtain from Hastings Street, from the old Deluxe Cinema, and it's a great big black, turning green, but gold letters, you know, four feet high the word DELUXE on it, and we said, Ah, that's what we'll call ourselves.*

It was how they became the Deluxe Brothers.

Roger Brewton lived on the flats for a while. His first shack was "actually a raft, and it would rise and fall with the tides. And it was very — the one I was in was really old, it had been out there for thirty or forty years when I got there," a remnant of a long history of squatting. Roger belonged to the Banana Brothers, a kind of "artist co-op, for lack of a better word in those days," he said. "It wasn't money or power or anything else" that motivated them; "it was just being creative, or at the moment." I wanted to know who made up his "family."

> *Marshall Mar, David Lowe, Russell Louie, and Rick Feldman. Greg Pickwell, and then we had Bob Mueller, famously known as the Buffalo, and then we had, you know, kind of an entourage, but they were all friends and family, but that was the core group.*

They were all jewellers and leathersmiths who had gotten to know each other in Gastown. All those men's names. I asked Roger if there were any women living with them on the mudflats. "Uh, yeah, there were a lot of women," he said,

> *mostly girlfriends, there weren't any women that actively came in together, we all came together and we had different businesses, and we amalgamated our businesses, in Gastown, and so all the ones that originally came together were all males at the time, not that we didn't want any women around but that's what happened ... they all had girlfriends, some of us, you know, during the duration.*

At the farthest east on the beach was a house where "The Boys" lived. Everyone I talked to mentioned "The Boys," a gang of young men undistinguished even by a "family name," as though they were suspended between childhood in their parents' abode and the familial conventions of married adulthood. "This group, what they called 'The Boys,'" Tom Burrows mused, "a floating, within the boys realm, this house would be anywhere from half a dozen to a dozen young, over-the-top hippies." There was a whole legend about these boys, and Tom laughed as he tried to recall it:

> Some, they, whatever, a couple of them made it to Peru — I can't believe all this happened in such a short period of time — Peru, and they got busted for having a joint in his pocket and put in a Lima jail, and when they were there they discovered cocaine, and they were shipping cocaine from the Lima jail back to a local post office, mounds of cocaine were arriving, which people had no idea — it wasn't around in the psyche then, they couldn't even place a value on it because there was no real market, and then the market took off, and a few of them made a lot of money out of it, to the point where they became movie producers.

Maybe this was after they lived on the mudflats, these "boys" with no names that had been mentioned to me.

And finally, at the other end of the spectrum, was Old Mike, last name Bozzer, the only remaining squatter from an earlier era. Like Lowry's "Manx boatbuilder," who "seemed to be the father or grandfather" of the fishermen squatters of a former generation, Bozzer was the revered "patriarch" of the extended "families" in the '70s. A resource worker who had lived on the Maplewood Mudflats since before Lowry's time, and who was a skilled worker of wood himself, Old Mike was considered, by squatters and officials alike, an almost legitimate resident by virtue of his longevity on the land. Roger Brewton of the Banana Brothers called Old Mike "a bit of an inspiration" to him and to others "because he was such a craftsman; most of us were craftsmen of some sort and liked traditional and older crafts."

Old Mike "had the old-style saws," Dan Clemens recalled. He wished he could draw me an illustration to show me how beautiful they were.

> He would lay these big draw saws out, you know the kind I'm talking about, big impressive teeth, with a handle on each end. You could take

his saw, and just lay it on top of a piece of wood and pull it once, and it would drop in there about three inches, you know. Beautiful beautiful sharpened saw blade.

Dan would go visit Old Mike at four in the morning; they'd drink some of Mike's dandelion wine together while Dan watched him cut his firewood with the fine old saws. The young guys would try to get firewood off the beach, "but we couldn't maintain it, or cut it, or we'd hit nails," so they bought all their firewood from Old Mike. "He kept us all going," Dan said, "but how he lived his life out there, almost subsistence living. He was no negative on anybody, he was simply a plus all the way."

Bridgeview

Bridgeview was no loose-knit scattering of makeshift shacks at the water's edge, but one of Surrey's oldest established neighbourhoods, dating back to the 1860s, before British Columbia even became a province. So why was it difficult for the local authorities to grant it the kind of swimming pool we were enjoying over in Kwantlen Park?

The community's future was "up in the air" because of the way it had developed over the previous century. By the 1890s there was a building boom as farmers in the Fraser Valley travelled by cart to bring their goods to the busy crossing point, where a regular ferry service funnelled eggs, produce, meat, and dairy products into New Westminster — whose position on the river ensured it a monopoly over the commercial trade in the Valley, giving Vancouver merchants stiff competition. That the Surrey side of the river was now known as "South Westminster" in itself signals that what was to become Bridgeview was at one time considered a kind of extension of the Royal City. With a hotel, a wharf, a small business district, and the Brownsville school, South Westminster must have had the quality of an integrated, bustling village, nestled against the river and flanked by the agricultural fields that fed its inhabitants.

The first bridge across the Fraser was built in 1904, a toll bridge with a lower level to serve the electric railway extending from Vancouver to the States, and an upper deck for foot and cart traffic. It was this bridge that ushered in the transportation surge that determined the fate of the neighbourhood just east of its Surrey access. Railways and eventually roadways converged at this point on the Fraser, and the Brownsville school closed, its students forced to attend a school farther south, some distance from the original neighbourhood. As roads improved and automobile traffic picked up, a second bridge was built in 1937, the two-lane Pattullo, and in 1940 the newly improved thoroughfare that fed it, coming up from the US border, received with much pomp and circumstance the name it had when I arrived: the King George Highway.

In riparian ecology, water erodes the shallow basin of a widening river channel as it meanders toward its coastal destination, sometimes forming a bar of sediment that, over time, extends out into the river. This bar may eventually cut off a section of flow, trapping a strip of water, called a slough, between sediment and shore. The residential section of South Westminster was becoming the dry-land version of a slough, with rail, truck, car, and barge traffic rushing by, but leaving a sediment of barriers to movement in the neighbourhood itself.

By the 1940s the residents had come to have a strong sense of themselves as a community, despite or perhaps because of the isolating factors that swirled around them, and in 1949, after much petitioning to Surrey council, a new elementary school was opened to serve the younger children there. Crossing the busy thoroughfare that the King George Highway had become was now too dangerous for them. The Surrey History website describes a contest that was held to name the new school. The winning entry, "Bridge View," signalled the area's relinquishment of its identification with New Westminster in favour of a name that emphasized one's perspective on the steel girders that seemed to separate it from, rather than connect it to, the rest of the world. "Bridge View" morphed into "Bridgeview" and eventually came to stand for the entire neighbourhood, though the bridge itself was visible to only a few of the residents.

As might be expected, the proliferating and ever-improved transportation channels drew more and more industry to the area, so that by the time my family moved into the motel, Bridgeview was completely surrounded by the noisy highway to its south, a hodgepodge of polluting industries along what used to be its access to the river, and busy thoroughfares on every side, allowing truck traffic to rumble by the houses and school on their way to and from the junkyards, sawmills, loading docks, and gravel pits that baffled the neighbourhood's peripheral vision. If you wanted to visit a doctor, do your grocery shopping, fill a prescription, go to high school, attend a hockey game; you had to find your way up Peterson Hill via the King George.

But it wasn't just social and economic services that had been subtracted from the Bridgeview community since its earlier days as part of South Westminster. It was also deficient in some of the basic amenities for survival that other suburban neighbourhoods took for granted: namely, a reliably functioning sewer system. Bridgeview families could get plenty of fresh water for drinking, cooking, and washing; they were deluged like everyone else by regularly falling precipitation throughout the year; the swollen Fraser ran nearby, albeit obscured by warehouses, smokestacks, and railyards. But when it came to the basic need to eliminate human waste, Bridgeview was, it seemed, haunted by its own feces.

This corner of Surrey had, like the rest of the municipality, been surveyed into a neat series of streets running perfectly north to south, east to west, divided and subdivided into a numbered grid, 114 Avenue, 114A Avenue, 114B Avenue, and so on. Newcomers to the area through the 1920s, the depression, the war, the 1950s dutifully built their one- and two-storey wooden and stucco bungalows along the pre-planned grid, trusting that improvements like street lights and road upgrades would come in time. Each home had its own septic tank to take care of effluent. Although that seemed to function okay for a while, by the early 1950s it was apparent that the spongy peat underlying the settlement did not offer the ideal conditions for this method of waste elimination. Every time it rained more than a little bit — and that was often in this part of the world — the water table rose dramatically, causing septic tanks to overflow, their contents seeping out into the rainwater ditches bordering every house. Even when the rain stopped, a buildup of sediment, backwash, and general trash prevented the ditches from draining properly.

In the early 1950s the problem must have been acknowledged by the local council because it promised to install sewers. But it delayed actually carrying out the promise. By 1966 the situation was so bad and coliform counts so high that health authorities put a freeze on all residential development in the area, pending an improvement in the sewage problem. The freeze was still in effect by the early '70s, when I began to volunteer for the Bridgeview drop-in centre. I didn't have a high opinion of the houses up in our neighbourhood around West Whalley Junior Secondary, with their makeshift carports, waterlogged wooden decks, and faux balconettes — but at least their owners were permitted to repair their roofs and replace rotting window sashes.

Not so down in Bridgeview, where, as the NFB film I found points out, a homeowner named Steve Putama "was still trying to get a permit to finish his house." The camera pans across a bungalow typical of the area, but half the house is obscured by a crisscross of boards slapped up, temporary scaffolding that had been there for years to support the structure while Putama waited. A ladder lies on the pitched roof, as though to hold the shingles on, and I'm put in mind of a photograph one of the Maplewood Mudflats squatters shared with me. Dan Clemens sent a black-and-white photo of his roomy shack, a one-time boomhouse that you could find "all over BC, you know, for boom guys [he meant the loggers who maintained the ubiquitous log booms up and down British Columbia's waterways], shacks for all of them to sit around and have coffee, you know, get out of the rain. Yup, I had one of those." He directed me to look at the photograph. "You'll see there's power lines coming into it, and little steps up to the power lines, I find that funny ... and there's a ladder on the roof for fixing the chimney and repairing the roof." This was what Steve Putama's unfinished house in

'Still trying to get a permit to finish his house.' Steve Putama's house. **Some People Have to Suffer**

Bridgeview reminded me of. But for Dan, the air of incompletion, of disrepair, the ramshackle look of the boomhouse, was part of its charm, its attraction, what made it "a very special place," as he put it. Like life, it was a work in progress, and the tools of the work were always on view. But what offered the appearance of chosen transience on the North Shore had the air of an imposed misery on the Bridgeview residential grid.

Putama was willing to abide by the rules; he went with his fellow residents, most of them homeowners, to confront the mayor and the aldermen and demand just the simplest thing: the infrastructure that would make their neighbourhood clean and safe again so that they could get back to the business of improvements on their private property. They did not spurn the very notion of property ownership as those artists on the North Shore seemed to be doing, so why was their status as tenuous as that of a squatter? It didn't seem right somehow.

The story was always in the local weekly newspapers. Those were the days when there were two such papers, rivals, who covered the hard news of the municipality, and they couldn't seem to decide which was funnier: these working-class rowdies, many of them recent immigrants with strong European accents, who persisted in living in a rat-infested cesspool, or the businessmen politicians whose evasions and prevarications, delays, and outright condescension no doubt masked their ties with developers who stood to make a lot of dough if the residential zone down by the bridge could be bought up and redeveloped for industrial and commercial use.

The headlines zigzagged back and forth as study after study focused on Bridgeview. In February 1971, homes were to "Remain Bridgeview's Core," but in October of that year there had been "Too Much Studying, No Final Decisions." In December 1971, residents urged "Riverfront for Public Use," and in April 1972, Bridgeview residents insisted their "Houses Will Stay." By October 1972, "Bridgeview Authorizes Drop-In Centre," culling volunteers from the nearby high schools — schools which my Bridgeview classmates found it hard to arrive at on time, especially in the rainy season. So in December 1972 "A Request for Buses for Bridgeview" was made, but in April 1973 "Bridgeview Busing Gets Turned Down." By the time we were coming up on Summer 1973, "Sewers Were Demanded [Again] in Bridgeview Area," and even though the "Majority of the Residents Say Yes to Sewers," and the authorities agreed that the "Ditches Cause Health Hazard," promising that the "Ditches Would Get Cleaned," by July the "Bridgeview Decision Was Set Back Two Weeks." Then there were to be "No Sewers for Bridgeview" because the "Sewer Proposal Was Down the Drain." And on and on it went.

As this drama unfolded for another few years, it was captured in the NFB film I had discovered, which was released in 1976. Even then the problem had not been entirely resolved. In the Maplewood Mudflats films, the fight with the North Vancouver District authorities takes the form of early morning outdoor standoffs on the mudflats themselves between bulldozer operators and agitated residents, looking the worse for wear after being roused from slumber by the sound of their neighbours' shack being flattened. While the mayor was interviewed for the films, he is never seen in the same frame as the squatters themselves. Not so for the Bridgeview film, where encounter after encounter was filmed in council chambers or other meeting rooms, with residents shown directly challenging the decision-makers in their municipality. After one such meeting, an alderman is interviewed, a middle-aged businessman by the name of Fred Beale. Those people down there, he says, are to be commended for their *esprit de corps*, but, you know, he was looking at it from the point of view of the municipality as a whole, and in a municipality of this size some people have to suffer, and it may be in this case that the people of Bridgeview have to suffer. *Some People Have to Suffer* — it became the title of the film.

Challenge for Change

But I'm getting ahead of myself here — bringing you passages from this film without filling in the background of how it came to be made in the first place. That is a worthy tale in itself and says a lot about how Bridgeview was taking shape not just as a residential neighbourhood beset by the kind of problems that attended urban development in the latter half of the twentieth century, but also as a poster child for wave upon wave of community development schemes. The drop-in centre where I had volunteered was one such program, targeting North Surrey, and Bridgeview in particular, as a deserving recipient of social intervention by well-meaning initiatives intended to improve the lives of the downtrodden.

When I received my DVD copy of *Some People Have to Suffer*, sent through the mail by the National Film Board (since it was not among the films that could be streamed on its extensive website), the first thing I did was to google Christopher Pinney, its director. Could he still be found somewhere? Had he made other films? When the search results came up, I got a thrill: he was as nearby as Boston, where he was on the faculty (at that time) of the Boston

College Carroll School of Management — blogging on the virtues of "corporate citizenship." In other words, close enough to where I lived in Rhode Island that I could interview him in person.

But what was he doing in the corporate world? Had he crossed over to the "other side"? This did not mesh with the film he had made some forty years earlier, where he documented the rising up of "the people" against a local government seemingly in cahoots with the corporate industrialization of a neighbourhood. Moreover, what I learned from him was that he was not just documenting but outright aiding and abetting the grassroots uprising depicted in his film. In reply to my inquiring email, surprised that I had tracked him down after all this time, he answered that yes, he did indeed direct the film about Bridgeview and "set up and ran the bigger project that it was a part of." And what project was that? I wondered. From there, a whole era of federally funded Canadian activist filmmaking opened up to me.

As it turned out, almost immediately after the year in which I

'And there's a ladder on the roof.' Dan Clemen's house. Michael de Courcy

volunteered at the Bridgeview drop-in program (and to this day I don't know whether it fizzled out or if I just quit, feeling that I had neither the talents nor the inclination to work with large groups of young children), another much more ambitious program began to take shape, in Surrey and Bridgeview in particular. This time it came all the way from Ottawa or, perhaps more properly, from Montreal, home of the federally funded National Film Board. The NFB was bringing what it called its Challenge for Change program to Canada's West Coast.

Some backstory here: In 1967 the NFB inaugurated a media experiment that involved sending newly trained "social animators" out to the far reaches of Canada to help local citizens solve their problems through movie and video activism. Social animation was a form of community organizing developed by Michel Blondin in Quebec, where Canada's marginalization of French language and culture, along with the post-industrial poverty crisis that the rest of the country was facing, led to a politicization of the province that was perhaps unique. In French, the concept of animation had long been used in educational, recreational, and entertainment contexts and meant something like facilitation, or the organization or leading of others in a learning experience, a sport, a group singalong, or a bus tour, for instance. Any activity you participated in as part of a group usually involved an *animateur* — indeed, had our drop-in been located in some down-and-out suburb of Montreal, we "super friends" might have been referred to as *animateurs*, as would my camp counsellors from the summer before.

The term began to have a more specialized meaning when linked with *sociale*, and *animateur sociale* came to signify what in the United States would be called a community developer. By the time the NFB adopted the concept, it had been translated wholesale into English as "social animator," which gave it a curious resonance it had not had in French, or so it feels to me. Surely the French did not envision a person being literally "animated" or put into motion by the *animateur*. For them the term must carry only the everyday sense of leading, organizing, facilitating, supervising.

But in English the term "social animator" evoked the image of a social group of otherwise passive or static people who were sparked, provoked, galvanized into action by their "animator." Except in rare pockets of activism, the term has not retained the popularity it had among community and media activists across Canada during the late '60s and '70s. In today's digital era, "social animator" refers not to real people acting in the world but to representations of people on a screen, animated for virtual social interaction in video games, and other digital deployments of moving avatars. In architectural parlance it refers to the means by which an aspect of a public building, say, provides structural support to "animate" the people who move through it by encouraging consumption (shops and cafes), entertainment (stages or arenas), etc. But hardly political action.

The experiment with film-based social animation started on the other side of the continent, in a community on Fogo Island, Newfoundland, where the fishing industry was in such dire straits that the federal government was proposing to solve the poverty problem there with a massive relocation scheme. The inhabitants of these fishing villages had prayed in their churches, studied in their schoolhouses, shopped in their local markets, and met in their community halls for more generations than even the residents of Bridgeview had; and they, too, were loath to leave their homes as part of a government-sponsored modernization project. NFB filmmaker Colin Low came to the villages on the island, and with the help of local community leaders he made a series of short films, each of which allowed the local residents to talk about how they saw the situation, what they perceived as obstacles to their needs, and pros and cons of various solutions.

Some films were simply windows onto the islanders' daily lives: a wedding, a group of kids building a fort near the water, a fisherman renovating a boat. Low arranged meetings at which the villagers could screen the films, which in turn formed the basis for discussion among them, the impetus to articulate their plight and make plans about how they might pressure the federal government for alternative solutions.

The Fogo Island series was the pilot project for the NFB's massive activist media experiment, dubbed Challenge for Change, which continued until 1985. Animators were sent to a Black neighbourhood in Halifax, where racism had reached alarming proportions; they were trained in a poor Montreal *quartier*, where residents were attempting to start their own health care centre; and they made videos in rural Alberta, where the mining industry had been faltering for years. By 1973, Challenge for Change was making its way to British Columbia, where Chris Pinney had just been assigned as the West Coast coordinator.

I wish I could say that in the next few years, as I transitioned to high school and then to the local college where Pinney and his cadre of social animators had set up a community communications centre, our paths crossed. And that NFB-sponsored media activism politicized me at a very early age. But it didn't quite happen that way. Almost as soon as I ceased to appear in Bridgeview as a teenage drop-in-centre volunteer, Chris Pinney drove across the Pattullo Bridge from his fairly recent residence in Vancouver (he was a transplant from back East) and scoped out the municipality as a likely locale in need of Challenge for Change. We never met.

Most of Canada's other Challenge for Change projects had focused on social issues such as poverty, racism, health care, First Nations struggles, and unemployment. Once a likely area had been targeted for intervention, social animators would be sent out to meet with groups of residents with the goal of identifying the most pressing problems to be solved. Since the program had been defined as based in the moving image, the idea was to explore how the demystification of mass media and the democratization of image making might facilitate social change in a way that truly benefited the least powerful.

As Portapak video technology became available, animators trained their citizens' groups in how to use the new equipment and how to exploit what everyone took to be its revolutionary potential. Ordinary people interviewed each other, covered the mundane business of community meetings, or captured the incriminating blather of a local politician on videotape; these were called "process videos," to be played back in meetings with other members of the community and used as the basis for further organization, further animation. Or the videos would be taken to the next municipal council meeting, or even brought up to the provincial level, and presented as evidence in an argument for funds, for legislation, for changes that local lawmakers had been otherwise reluctant to make.

It will be no surprise to the reader of this saga of eviction narratives set on Vancouver's waterfront fringes, with its history of squatters, shifting river deltas, disappearing forests, shrinking agricultural land, displaced First Nations, clashes between working-class homeowners and municipal politicians looking to make a buck from industrial development, that Chris Pinney and his local animators decided to define Challenge for Change in terms of "land use" in British Columbia. And while they had minor satellites going in the hinterlands of the province, they made Surrey the hub of their activity, since the vast municipality seemed to function as a microcosm of the diversity of land-use problems that beset the province in general.

Literally dozens of process videos were made, documenting the shoddy workmanship on a housing development where corners had been cut to deliberately undermine a federal funding scheme, gathering angry reactions from local residents where a petrochemical plant had been planned, laying out the ecological impact of a proposed sanitary landfill on a precious marshland along the Fraser, or documenting the sub-par conditions in an apartment building, then offering a blueprint for starting a co-op, thereby circumventing the necessity for a landlord. Mostly half-inch, reel-to-reel videos, these fragile windows onto a fleeting decade in the history of Surrey, and the history of media activism, sit in boxes in one of the local college archives today. They may have degraded beyond the point where they could be viewed anymore, even if you could find the equipment to watch them. But because a few were edited onto three-quarter-inch video for broadcast on public access cable television, they were easily transferred to DVD and gave me an inkling of what was going on in my municipality, a taste of what the animators were animating — and just how many industrial or dump sites were averted.

But Pinney also made a longer, enduring film during this period — the one I found on the NFB's "films for purchase" website when I was searching for images of the look and feel of Surrey in the '70s. That film was, of course, the Bridgeview ditch and sewer drama, *Some People Have to Suffer.*

Pinney's posse of social animators — Jim Gillis, a local businessman; Jim Sellers, who taught at the newly opened Douglas College; and Norma Taite, who was building a house with her husband down in White Rock — began to make contact with some of the parents, no doubt, of the kids I had been a "super friend" to at the drop-in. It must not have taken long for Chris, Norma, and the Jims to figure out that what Bridgeview needed was not a few well-intentioned teenagers from up the hill to play volleyball and crab soccer with their kids after school hours (though a broad-based childcare program would have been beneficial to everyone in Surrey), but a functional sewer system to take away their wastewater, and, in the meantime, a thorough cleaning of the rainwater ditches in which rats dodged empty cigarette packages as they swam through the green scum from one clogged culvert to another.

What distinguished the Challenge for Change initiative from our drop-in program in Bridgeview was not just a shift in emphasis, from social betterment to improved material conditions, but an influx of serious funding. It was the era of generous Liberal spending at the federal level under Prime Minister Pierre Trudeau's leadership, with programs like Opportunities for Youth, Neighbourhood Improvement, and Residential Rehabilitation Assistance. But in BC the funnelling of government money to progressive social policies was intensified with the election of the New Democratic Party led by Dave Barrett in 1972. From my perspective, the election of this left-wing visionary to head up what I was coming to think of as "our" province, followed by the crashing disappointment of Nixon's re-election down in the States, was helping me feel marginally better about having left the known American world for this Canadian backwater. At least I could feel good about the politicians who were running things.

What was extraordinary about the Challenge for Change program in Surrey, as I look back on it from today's perspective, is that a filmmaker in the employ of the federal government (for Pinney was, indeed, a "government employee" insofar as his paycheques came from the National Film Board, a government agency, just like the Manpower Office and the postal service) was entrusted, with his team, to size up the most pressing needs of the common people of the province, and then, having come up with the category that would cover the widest range of issues they had targeted, to draft plans of action to "animate" the citizenry, with the help of video cameras, to get what they needed. To do this, Pinney prepared reports and proposals, each of them laying out a budget for a given local project, and managed to secure not only federal money from the NFB itself, but tens of thousands of dollars from the provincial government as well. With proper funding like this, he was able to pay the animators a regular, if modest, wage; purchase cameras, videotape, film, projectors, monitors, and editing equipment; and establish a work base for his team: a trailer on the newly established Douglas College campus — cramped, but big enough to house equipment, edit film, and give locals lessons on how to operate the Portapak video cameras they would need to document the land-use conflicts that most affected them.

It wasn't so much that as soon as the NFB arrived on the scene, with its cameras and clout, Surrey's mayor and council relented and agreed to provide the much-needed infrastructure to Bridgeview residents. The battle continued to be long and drawn out. But the animators put those federal and provincial dollars to good use, coaching the Bridgeview residents in how to locate just the correct pressure points in local council, who to bring in at the provincial level, how to make sure their interests were represented at committee and council meetings, and, perhaps most importantly, how to ensure that every step along the way was documented on video.

The residents videotaped hours and hours of meetings, *animateur* Norma Taite told me when we met, because you just never knew what might be needed, what they might want to do with it later.

Some of the fuzzy black-and-white video footage was incorporated into Pinney's finished documentary, along with colour film footage of the ramshackle houses; the brackish ditchwater; trucks whooshing by schoolchildren in their damp parkas, swinging their empty lunch pails; a shot of an industrial concern of some kind, with acres of colourful storage drums in the foreground, drab houses in the middle ground, and the orange Pattullo Bridge off in the distance. Talking heads abound, especially the mealy-mouthed aldermen, mayor, and industrial planner, rationalizing why it was so hard to help those Bridgeview people given the conditions of the soil and the fact that land was cheap — and why shouldn't the developers buy it? It's not fit for residential living anyway. Community leader Otto Wittenberg was interviewed, along with his neighbour Alice Wilcox, with her wry smile and wire-framed sunglasses. They stand in a weedy field, one of Bridgeview's vacant lots that had recently been bought. Otto refers to a map he has that shows "umpteen dozens of holding companies that have bought in here ... all the biggies." When Pinney comments that the area is not supposed to be worth anything, Wittenberg agrees and adds, "But then the mayor's turned around, or not the mayor himself, but his brother, and they bought this piece of property that we're standing on, and they paid the fantastic price of a hundred thousand dollars for it."

Alice adds that she didn't think any land in Bridgeview could be valued at such a price "because everyone has told us that the land has no value, and the sooner people move out, the better it will be for them."

In the next scene a nonchalant Mayor Vander Zalm is interviewed, defending the rights of "these real estate people" to "go in there," since the land is a good investment. "That's the system, it's permitted, it's allowed." But whether in fact "this is council's fault, no, I don't agree," he concludes, as though the "real estate people"

'Everyone has told us that the land has no value.' Bridgeview activists Otto Wittenberg and Alice Wilcox. **Some People Have to Suffer**

and the council members have nothing to do with each other.

What you couldn't tell by watching the film was that, according to one of Chris Pinney's reports, Norma and the Jims had been doing some serious animating in the background, helping Otto and Alice investigate "all land purchases and turnover in Bridgeview in the last ten years" to determine "whether or not land speculators will be the prime beneficiaries" of the latest program proposed by the municipality. These were "super friends" to Bridgeview, indeed.

In a grainy black-and-white video sequence, Vander Zalm, with his Dudley Do-Right chin, bow tie, and leisure jacket, fiddles with a pencil, at a loss what to say when a strongly accented voice confronts him from offscreen.

"Who put the freeze on us? Who?" it demands.

"Uh, damned if I ... uh ..." The mayor doesn't seem to have a clue.

Was that Steve Putama, wanting to know when the ban on permits would be lifted so that he could finally put the roof on his house? The camera cuts to another man who pops up from his chair now, long sideburns, rumpled hair, aviator glasses, and a work jacket. He asks, "If you can't get a permit from the Boundary

'Council's fault? No, I don't agree.' Surrey Mayor Bill Vander Zalm. *Some People Have to Suffer*

**BILL VANDER ZALM
Mayor of Surrey**

Health Unit, then why are we living in the house?" The mayor can't answer that one either, and as a general hubbub sets in, another anonymous voice can be heard just above the fray, not a Bridgeviewer, but not an opponent either: "We should not, I suppose, be letting people live here, but you're living here, so we have to do something, we have to clean it up." And now all hell seems to break loose, with unintelligible voices crying out from all directions, heads jerking and hands gesticulating in the crowded room. It was grainy sequences like these, taken as process videos, that provided Chris Pinney with the most dynamic footage for the film he was piecing together.

Shacking Up

Back on the North Vancouver mudflats there were these egalitarian "families" of artisans and their girlfriends, there were "the boys," there was the veteran beachcomber pensioner, respected for his practical life knowledge, and then there were more conventional family units, like the Spongs: a scientist father, a housewife mother, a kid. Paul and Linda were, perhaps, closest in affinity with another three-member family — the artist Tom Burrows, his Italian wife, Ida (pronounced *Eeda*), and their toddler, Elisha. While Paul studied meditators hooked up to monitors in his laboratory at UBC, and Tom constructed and refined his Malevich-style sculptures in the mud, Linda and Ida looked after the little boys, and a friendship developed between the two young families.

Oddly, they shared an origin story where their mudflats residency was concerned. In both cases it was during a rocky period of separation in each couple's married life that Tom and Paul were drawn to the mudflats, though they did not know each other then. Linda had left Paul and was living with a friend when he purchased, for a few hundred dollars, the "whorehouse" on the mudflats that he made his home. Tom's story came out when he met me in the artist "work/live" studio near Gastown that he now called home for part of the year — when he's not on Hornby Island, where he had a grander version of a mudflats-style structure built in the years after his eviction.

He had been living in London in the late '60s — "pretty bohemian wild times" he called it — and had just reached the end of his postgraduate scholarship. Things were "taking off" for him, he told me. "But I had a really rocky marriage, and part of the rocky marriage ... I also had a child on the way." He described his panicked response to this "family" starting up, a family he was not sure he was ready for: "I went off on my birthday with [artist] friend ... Jerry Pethick, we went on a binge and ended up after a day or so driving my post office van to Heathrow airport, going to New York, and we were there for, oh, three or four, five days, and finally we kind of walked out of our crazy binge with nothing, homeless."

Tom made it from New York up to Ontario, where he painted houses to make enough money to move back to Vancouver. He had gotten his undergraduate degree at UBC and had been to the mudflats during his university days — it was where his hash dealer, Peter Choquette, lived.

> *I always loved his living environment, so I kind of went there, and here was this empty platform I went on, and started building on it, and*

he showed up, demanded some form of compensation, even though it wasn't his, and so I paid him something, didn't want to argue, just kept building, and in September my wife showed up with a child, which I hadn't seen since before he was born, when I was away.

It was a variant of the immigrant tale, or perhaps a twentieth-century pioneer story — where the patriarch goes forth in search of land in the new world of the Wild West, stakes his claim, then is followed by the wife and child. Though in this case it was only in retrospect that a panicked fugue state could be reinterpreted as a scouting mission to set up a homestead for the rest of the family unit.

What struck me about this double story is that in both cases the couple married to begin with, but as they approached the '70s — the decade in which I came of age — the marriage had begun to sour. By reuniting in a makeshift squatter's dwelling on the mud-flats, were they retrospectively "shacking up" with each other? Performing a do-over in a liminal space that might in some way reset the mechanism that had gone awry? What moved people to live as squatters in the first place? Was it a utopian impulse?

When I asked Tom Burrows this question, he seemed skeptical. At some points it's utopian, he conceded. But sometimes it's necessity, and sometimes just comfort. For him, he said, it was an ideal situation while it lasted.

What made it ideal?

The tide going in and out, he said.

We had just been talking about how the tide became an intrinsic component in his sculpture, the very medium in which he was working at that time. "So was the ideality of the flats defined in terms of your work," I asked, wanting to know more about an intertidal aesthetics, an artistic principle premised on water that would rise underneath you, as though to float you away at any moment. It was an invitation to talk more about what made his art tick in those days. But the word "work" seemed to switch him to another topic altogether, or perhaps to the "opposite" side of his work at the time: "Yeah, in terms of my work and also in terms . . ." he paused, "— yeah, I guess it was in terms of my work. I guess if I was a good young dad I would have ..." But he couldn't finish that sentence. What had he thought I was asking about then? What doubts did he have about his fathering?

"In the NFB film," I offered, "Paul Spong says the mudflats were the best place to raise children."

"Uh." Tom again seemed dubious. "It can be slightly dangerous." He chuckled, as though at a private joke.

I pressed on: "Paul gave the impression that it was a place to find refuge from danger. You didn't have to worry about your kid getting hit by a car, for example."

"There were different kinds of danger." He laughed again, then, "I remember at one point liberating some snow fencing from by the side of the road and creating this corral that we could put our kids in so they didn't have to be in diapers, 'cause the tide would come in and take it away," he recalled.

I pictured the bare-assed toddlers, running around inside the thin slats of the snow fencing. "So," I said, "the tide was the diaper-changer." And who was looking after all these kids?

"Pretty much the ... things were ... liberation hadn't really gotten hold."

"Hadn't made it as far as the mudflats?"

"Yeah, it was, you know, it was just, the whole women's lib thing was just beginning on the academic level. I mean, it's been around forever, but that resurgence was very powerful there, but it hadn't quite got out to the semi-rural spaces."

"Well, then," wanting to know more about that particular "semi-rural" space, "what was it like, having kids at that age, in that environment?" I meant looking after toddlers on the mudflats.

"It was ... they were around," Tom said vaguely — meaning the kids, I presume. "I was pretty bad. I preferred the Cecil Hotel. At that time the Cecil Hotel was a wonderful university environment."

"Where you would go and meet with people?"

"Yeah, on the way home [from the University of British Columbia]."

The Cecil Hotel, I knew, was legendary, remembered as the

artistic and intellectual hub of Vancouver in the early '70s. It's where lefty *Vancouver Sun* journalist Bob Hunter met with his even more radical colleagues Dan McLeod and Bob Cummings, who had founded Vancouver's independent paper, the *Georgia Straight*, during meetings at the Cecil. As Vancouver writer George Bowering remembered it, "We poets went to the Cecil around 10 PM, after the college boys had got lucky or drunk and gone home or elsewhere." In a commemorative blog, Vancouver resident Janet Mackie called the Cecil a congregation place for "poets and writers and potters and artists and musicians and bar-room philosophers and existentialist cab-drivers and Malcolm Lowry fans and alcohol-impaired Ph.D.s and fine-arts majors turned carpenters." It was a convenient midpoint between the university neighbourhoods of Point Grey and Kitsilano, and the working-class district of the east side, according to Rex Weyler. The original activists of what was to become Greenpeace met at the Cecil — indeed, it was here, after Spong's debacle with the Vancouver Aquarium, that "the intelligentsia crowd toasted the diminutive scientist as a visionary." Linda had mentioned the Cecil too, where she said "a lot of stuff happened," where art and politics entered the public sphere from the ambience of the public watering hole. As a friend had remarked to her not so long before: "None of this would have happened if they hadn't been drinking so much beer." At the Cecil Hotel, she meant.

But I hadn't heard the Cecil referred to in quite this sheepish way before — as though Tom was owning up to some sort of crime he had committed. He knew the kids were "around" the mudflats, but he didn't see much of them first-hand, I'm gathering now, since he spent most of his time at the Cecil, enjoying its university ambience. Preferring the Cecil was tantamount to being "pretty bad" in retrospect, not what you would call a "good young Dad."

The Return of Malcolm Lowry

Round the point northwards beyond the seaport were indeed miles of muddy flats at the lowest tides with old pilings like drunken giants bracing each other up, as if staggering homeward evermore from some titanic tavern in the mountains.
— Malcolm Lowry, 'THE FOREST PATH TO THE SPRING'

Maybe it was someone like Tom Burrows that Janet Mackie was thinking of when she included among her list of Cecil Hotel regulars "Malcolm Lowry fans." More than a fan, Tom saw in Lowry a kind of spiritual predecessor — the artist squatter who had gone before. Indeed, where squatting was concerned, there was almost a direct line of descent from Lowry to Burrows: Lowry had been friends with Vancouver poet Earle Birney, who had been a teacher of Tom's when he switched his major, as an undergraduate, from medicine to creative writing. Only two degrees of separation. If the flats were a place for the expression of paternal relations, it was not blood relations that interested Tom, it would seem, but artistic relations.

This connection with Lowry became the basis of a fleeting art installation. One October evening in 1970, Vancouver commuters going across the Second Narrows Bridge, which spans Burrard Inlet just west of the Maplewood Mudflats, might have glimpsed what appeared to be an animated male nude walking swiftly across the bridge toward the mountains on the North Shore — as though a pale ghost was making his way, with the haste of a refugee, from the city to his shack on the shore. *Bridge Walk*, Burrows called it, a.k.a. *The Return of Malcolm Lowry.*

I'm describing this silvery figure from a pinkish photograph snapped through the windshield of a passing car, Burrows's photo-documentation of the performance. I didn't understand at first what I was looking at, the walker is so smooth and featureless, though the sun, hidden offscreen to the west, throws its shadow onto the bridge's green railing. Is that a piece of statuary, I asked, or a person? "It's me," Tom said.

> *I'm covered in silver, I've got a cap on and trunks, walking across quite mechanically, across Second Narrows Bridge at rush hour so anyone checking on it can't go back 'cause you have to keep going, and then I was picked up and taken away quickly at the other end.*

The commuters would not have known who or what this bridge-walker was; only if you were to see the photographic record on display in a gallery, with its accompanying artist's statement, would you learn that since its opening in 1960,

> *the Second Narrows Bridge, with constricted linearity and regimented speed of transit, was the major artery from the urban core of Vancouver to the amorphous open nature of the north shore tidal flats. Burrows (the sculptor) moved into a self-built squatter cabin on the north shore Maple Wood tidal flats in June of 1969.*

The Return of Malcolm Lowry was meant to resonate with *The Return of Martin Guerre*, a film which had "just come out," according to Burrows. But it seemed to me that something was off in that chronology. Turns out the film was not released until 1982. Perhaps Burrows had titled his performative sculpture *Bridge Walk* in 1970, then added the subtitle in the 1980s, when Gérard Depardieu played the imposter who, in the seventeenth century, claimed to be a woman's husband returning from a many years' absence in the wars. His wife at first welcomes him, as do the rest of the villagers, but little by little they come to doubt that he is the same man who left the village, until, in the end, he is put on trial for duping them all, for not being who they wanted him to be, the real Martin Guerre.

Burrows is the imposter in *Bridge Walk*, a ghostly Lowry striding back as though from the library in Enochvilleport, as he called Vancouver, which he detested for its inhospitable bars and its soulless urban improvement schemes. Or maybe from the Niagara Hotel, Lowry's Cecil, where he'd have a few drinks before returning to his writing table on the water. Burrows as Lowry walks back to the mudflats nude but not naked exactly, what with the silver finish and the trunks, returning, perhaps, to a wife who would welcome him whether or not he was the man she married, to live with her on the outskirts of North Vancouver, like Martin Guerre in his village,

Tom Burrows, BRIDGE WALK, 1970. Collection of the Morris and Helen Belkin Art Gallery, University of British Columbia, Tom Burrows fonds.

until mistrust and suspicion begin to fester, his status shaky, shifting, then challenged. Then brought to trial, along with the other squatters, for living illicitly among those who belong.

"Did you feel you had a continuity with Lowry," I asked, "with where he had lived, and with his relation to his work?"

"Sort of," Tom said. "I felt a fellow alcoholic, anyway."

Bridge Walk suggests an alternative two degrees of separation from Lowry — not an artistic lineage, but the lineage of eviction. For I've left out half the artist's statement. It concluded:

> The same career municipal employee who bulldozed Malcolm Lowry's squatter home on a tidal area adjacent to the Maple Wood flats in 1954, organized the burning of the Burrows cabin in Dec. 1971.

Moreover, a postscript added, Lowry's first squatter cabin "burned in 1944 incinerating the fourth draft of *Under the Volcano*." In 1970, when he performed his Lowry revival, Burrows could not have known yet that his own cabin on the flats would suffer the same fate as that of his alcoholic forefather. It was only in retrospect that this inhabitation of the Lowry legacy would be officially consecrated, as it were, by the same human hand that had been responsible for the destruction of Lowry's shack. "I thought that was quite an honour," Burrows said.

The abstract mud-sculptures made of salvage, the performance of Bridge Walk — those were only the most obvious aspects of Burrows's "work" as an artist. It was the fact of squatting itself that constituted not just the context for these discrete constructions, but Burrows's very life-as-art in this period of time. The inhabitation of a shack on the shore, yes, but also the re-inhabitation of Lowry's prior tenancy in Dollarton seemed necessary, as though a Vancouver artist — and particularly one who had spent his formative years, as Burrows did, in England, the mother country from which Lowry was first evicted — could never really "come to life" without submitting himself to the muddy shifting sands of Lowry's squatter's existence on the city's littoral. Moreover, one could not willingly depart one's squatted shack, move on to a legitimate dwelling, and give in to the universals of taxes and sewer systems. For squatting to count as an act of deliberation, one had to push one's illegitimacy to its crisis and call into question the very grounds of legitimation in the first place. To be evicted by the same man who evicted Malcolm Lowry — this was an honour indeed. North Vancouver District's Inspector was the living link between Lowry and Burrows, a wizard whose magic touch, or rather torch, setting fire to a makeshift shack, lit the way for the next phase of Burrows's career.

Otto Jr.

I don't remember how it happened, but I think I told one of my childhood friends about this book, and perhaps I showed her *Some People Have to Suffer*, and maybe seeing Otto Wittenberg in the film jogged her memory. She wasn't sure, but she thought that one of our mutual friends knew the Wittenberg family, or knew Otto's son anyway, Otto Jr. I followed up on her lead and sure enough, although Otto Sr. had died some time ago, Otto Jr., my own age (we had gone to the same senior secondary school, but I didn't remember him), was still living nearby and was willing to talk about those Bridgeview days.

According to Otto Jr., the citizen petitions to city council had begun some years before the NFB arrived with its social animators. The earliest Otto was aware that his neighbourhood had a beef with the mayor and aldermen was back in 1970 or '71 (soon after we had arrived from the States). His family lived in a house on 116th Avenue, which at the time was called Industrial Avenue — whether in anticipation of the industrialization of the area or because it led to some already industrialized sector, I'm not sure. We both laughed at the name of his avenue in this ostensibly residential area. Up the street from his house, another family had repaired their leaky roof. But as soon as they repaired it, "they promptly got fined by the city." Could that have been Steve Putama, I asked, the same guy the film shows? No, that was a different family — there were many of them.

But in any case, that was his earliest memory, this fine slapped on his neighbour, and his understanding of it was that the city council, in order to artificially suppress the land values, had put a ban on improvements or repairs to property. This was what started things off, he said, and from there a "little bit of a fight-back committee started, and it got into a 'while we're at it,' and 'while we're doing this, we also need sewer service.'" I said I'd heard about the ban on improvements, that "freeze" referred to in the film, brought in by health authorities back in the '60s. It turned out I was wrong in thinking that Bridgeview had no problem getting fresh water. According to Otto, one of the amenities they sought, in addition to a proper sewer system, was more reliable water delivery. "At the time, we were getting our water from a wooden pipe that was attached to the railway bridge underneath the Pattullo," Otto explained. Things were even worse than I had realized.

Otto told me a bit about how his family came to live in Bridgeview, and as I mull it over now, I see that their story is a kind of counterpoint to the fanciful image of the "immigrant tale" I had conjured to characterize the arrival of Paul Spong and Tom Burrows on the Maplewood Mudflats, setting up house to make things ready before their wives and babies arrived. Otto Sr. had come to Canada from Germany in 1954, followed by his wife in 1956, and Otto Jr. "showed up," as he put it, the very next year. This was, in fact, the classic immigrant experience, I realized, not a facsimile of it. The Wittenbergs had a rented apartment in Port Moody at first, north of the Fraser, before buying their house in Bridgeview when Otto was five — "for thirteen thousand dollars, can you imagine that?"

As cheap as that might seem, this was no squatter's arrangement. And yet, the setting had charms reminiscent of those experienced up on the Maplewood Mudflats. There was that rather urban view from one's house across a nearby body of water, for instance — only in Otto's case it wasn't the nocturnal glow of a refinery he watched from his bedroom window, but the crisscross logo of the Lucky Lager sign at the brewery across the Fraser. And in the daytime, with a pair of binoculars, he could observe the inmates at the BC Penitentiary tending their vegetable gardens or feeding the livestock. "At that time, they did their own farming within the prison grounds," Otto said.

When they first moved to Bridgeview in the early '60s, it hadn't yet been completely encircled by industry. Out on the King George Highway there was the Turf Hotel (which I remembered, with its neon thoroughbred and jockey — it's still there today) and the Burger King. On the waterfront there was a gypsum plant, and the railway track that ran between their house and the river. Other than that, from the plant to the Pattullo Bridge, "it was just trees, shrub, and beach." All they had to do was put a "nice big board over the drainage ditch" in their backyard, cross over the train tracks, and "away we were, at the beach every day. That part was cool." I asked if that was why his dad moved them to Bridgeview, because of its proximity to the natural setting of the river's edge. "Well, could be," Otto said. But also, the neighbourhood was close to where his dad was going to be working, at Timberland Mill in neighbouring

South Westminster. Bridgeview was a lot closer to Timberland than Port Moody would have been. And Bridgeview was one of the few places where his parents could afford a house of their own. It was as simple as that.

Little by little, industry closed in on them as the '60s wore on. "Here and there a house was torn down, and strange businesses showed up." He recalled one place in particular, you could see it in the film, some sort of operation that involved storage barrels. "It was very close to Alice Wilcox's place," he said. "What was in these barrels, I don't know. You gotta wonder, like, you have a residential community, and you allow this to go into the middle of it?" And on another occasion there was "threat of expropriation of property by the railroad. Quite a lot of houses under threat of expropriation. So that was playing itself out at the same time, the community had basically several fronts at once." It was what galvanized them as a community, in fact. "And made them very tough to deal with, right?"

What I needed to know, he stressed, was that although the NFB animators might have been helping out by '73 or '74, "the game was pretty much already rolling when they got involved." Was that because there was such a strong sense of community among the Wittenbergs and Alice Wilcox and the other Bridgeview residents? No. In fact, it was kind of the other way around. It was the problems they had to deal with as a group that galvanized them, that brought them together.

Otto asked if I remembered the talk-radio show at the time, hosted by Jack Webster, on CKNW. Yes, of course, I said, though I hadn't heard this name in decades. Webster was known to be a pioneer of the talk-radio format in the '60s, and was even called on, in 1963, to act as a mediator between prisoners at the BC Pen and authorities during a hostage incident, right across the river from Otto's bedroom window. But this wasn't what Otto was talking about. By the early '70s, he said, Jack Webster had gotten involved in the plight of the Bridgeview residents. The whole sewer debacle was featured on the radio show quite a few times.

So this thing started to get a life of its own. People, the community, just basically realized they wanted to be a community, we wanted our houses fixed, not torn down, we wanted to live here, you know.

In the council minutes I see evidence of Bridgeview residents at City Hall in July 1970, for instance, when Alderman Rita Johnston brought to the council's attention a petition concerning the conundrum the residents faced in the decision-making process about the fate of their neighbourhood. "Any plebiscite would work against them irregardless of which way they vote," Johnston reported. "The petitioners say that if they vote for the area to be zoned industrial, they are in fact saying it is not satisfactory for homes and this would affect the sale of their properties. If they vote to have it declared residential, they have been advised that the cost of sewers is prohibitive. They also feel that their area has been downgraded over the years, and they suggested that Council take a closer look at their problems." Although this was two years before the NFB animators

'What was in these barrels, I don't know.' Industry and residential in Bridgeview. Some People Have to Suffer

arrived, Bridgeview seemed to have a pretty good grasp of the paradox it was facing.

Otto recalled one occasion when his father's gathering of anything and everything that might be useful as "evidence" on their behalf paid off in a particularly comical incident. Otto didn't know exactly how it started, but his parents had put a "little microphone device on their phone, so it would record stuff." One day Mayor Bill Vander Zalm was being interviewed by Jack Webster on his radio show, so they recorded the show with the phone recording device — it was a big reel-to-reel machine, "one of those great boxes we used to use back then." That night they went to a packed meeting at City Hall, really well attended, with people pressing in from outside.

> And Vander Zalm had made the comment on the radio that he just really didn't understand what it was that the citizens of this community wanted, right? Just playing the innocence card, if you will. And so when he was challenged on that at the meeting, he said, uh, that's not what he said. You know, like he denied it absolutely. Of course he knows what the citizens want, right?

At this point, Otto Sr. turned to his son and said, "Here's the keys, go to the trunk of the car, bring the tape recorder in."

We laughed together, knowing what was coming.

"So I hauled the beast of a thing in, and Vander Zalm sees it coming in, and he says, 'Okay, I may have said that,' he just backtracked like crazy. And for me, it was a very powerful lesson."

But what did Otto mean, that they didn't feel they were a community before they were galvanized by their persecution at the hands of city council? He tried to explain: his mother and father, they didn't really have much in the way of associations with their neighbours before the "Bridgeview Committee thing got going."

> And of course my mum couldn't speak English. She was German, both my parents were German, right? So there was a language barrier, and then there was just plain old life, and work, and my mum stayed home for most of the time, and she just did a lot of regular stuff, you know, running a garden, canning, and all that stuff that used to be

'It's nearly hate. They're creating it.' Otto and Moggel Wittenberg. *Some People Have to Suffer*

done in the old days, make your own bread, make your own this, make your own that. So that kind of didn't really lend itself so much to community.

Something was ringing in my ears at this point: Linda Spong's voice saying "I come from Los Angeles. When I came to Vancouver I was thrilled, like, 'these streets don't even have curbs, we must be making homemade bread soon!'" For Linda, homemade bread was a symbol of the utopian hippie dream of going back to the land. For Otto's mum, though, it was a continuation of just plain old life and work as she knew it, the "regular stuff" one did as a wife and mother with a house of her own and a plot of land fertile enough to allow for a family garden.

I pointed out that Otto's mum spoke English quite well by the time she was interviewed in *Some People Have to Suffer*, and in fact made some of the most forceful points, though she was not, alas, identified by name the way her husband was.

The two of them are shown sitting on the sofa in their living room, that same living room where most of the Bridgeview Committee meetings were held, Otto Jr. told me. We've seen some of the behaviour of the politicians in the film, their patronizing tones, their prevarications, both during council meetings and in talking-head interviews. Otto's mum leans forward on the couch, as though struggling to figure out something that is obscure. "When I see the aldermen, I respect them for what they are," she says. "But if I look at how they act, especially [towards] these people here in Bridgeview, they really look down on them." It frustrated her "just to approach them and talk to them," she says, referring to the council members. "And that is wrong. You should be able to talk about things. And we are not the enemy of City Hall. It's the opposite. They are ... it's their fault, that feeling, and I would say it's nearly hate. They're creating it."

This willful impulse on the part of those elected officials to deliberately produce "hate" in their constituents, that is what seemed to trouble her the most. Normally, she says, "I'm a very good-natured woman, I'm more on the soft side." But this condescension by City Hall, it's as though it produces something in her that is not recognizable, something harsher, harder. "I don't know what I would be able to do," she says.

> *All the people want to do is to live. What's wrong with it? ... Everybody wants to have his home, raise his family, be happy. And it's a nice place to live in. It's not expensive, I mean up the hill it's nice and maybe they have bigger houses, but I personally think I have a happy house, and it counts more.*

Women's Lib

Now I'm thinking more about this whole idea of the women's movement and where it was in my Western Canadian youth. Decades into my adult life it seemed like I had been a feminist all my life, hadn't I? Or was there a period when I "came to consciousness," as they say; when the scales began to fall from my eyes?

Women's liberation was, of course, a staple of the popular media — distorted, but at least part of common parlance. Think of *The Mary Tyler Moore Show*, for instance, which was a favourite in our household.

The *Vancouver Sun*, delivered daily to our motel, weighed in on this question of the battle of the sexes. Now, poring through a folder of clippings from the *Sun* on the Maplewood Mudflats squatters, I come across a page that coincidentally juxtaposes the bleak winter story of their imminent eviction with a reflection on sexual chauvinism. Featured is a huge photo of a dejected Tom Burrows wearing gumboots and toque, his toddler Elisha in a plaid parka straddling his right hip; they stand among Tom's sculptures, their shack a few yards behind, a desolate layer of December snow blanketing the sorry scene. Burrows claims to be living in "no man's land" the caption tells us, and there is a whole legalistic story behind that — it was Tom's futile last bid to dodge the bulldozers. But what interests me about this clipping is the Bob Hunter column included by happenstance on the left side of the page.

Bob Hunter, you may recall, was one of the regulars at the Cecil Hotel. He had for some time been writing a thrice-weekly column for the *Sun* as the paper's most left-wing commentator, mostly on environmental issues. He was just starting to help get the Greenpeace movement off the ground as one of its founding members. But on this day his column wasn't about oil spills or Alaskan nuclear blasts. It was about the "female chauvinist pig," who was, according to Hunter, "everywhere."

> One sees her in offices, on buses, in cars, airplanes, flouncing along the street in her outrageous costumes with paint all over her face. Not a few of these female sexists are indistinguishable from a drag queen.

He had decided, it appeared, to weigh in on "the whole women's lib thing," and to make a point he thought we had all missed: that if men were guilty of wielding their patriarchal power, then women were just as culpable for having "cornered the market" on "manipulation." Why else did "they have all that crap on their faces" or "put on giddy outfits whose sole function seems to be stimulation of the opposite sex?" Hunter admitted that, as Germaine Greer and Kate Millett had pointed out, this kind of sexual provocation was partly due to "brainwashing and conditioning," partly a "survival tactic.

"*The female chauvinist pig is everywhere.*" Bob Hunter column in the VANCOUVER SUN. Tom and Elisha Burrows, 'Mud Flat Squatter,' SUN, *December 10, 1971, p. 25.* Collection of the Morris and Helen Belkin Art Gallery Archives, the University of British Columbia, Tom Burrows fonds.

Barred from the corridor of power, women are forced for the most part to make it as prostitutes. Marriage, perhaps as often as not, is at some level a form of legalized prostitution." But, Hunter insisted, the real reason for all the "hot pants and false eyelashes and wigs and perfume" was that women assumed men were such "dumb, panting brutes" that they could be easily "herded down the chute like cattle." He wanted them to know that he, for one, preferred to deal "with human beings, not electric life-sized Barbie Dolls."

This muckraking nonsense was, in part, a provocation for women to submit their own takes on the feminist movement. And indeed, for a couple of columns after that, Hunter stepped aside and published an array of arguments by local feminists, from the Women's Liberation Alliance, who contributed what Hunter called a "knee-jerk political response," to a "more measured" letter, in his opinion, by Melanie Salutin, who advocated that women interested in liberation might start by joining one of the "rap groups" being formed in the city, where "women talk together about their most intimate feelings and experiences, learning to replace competitiveness with trust, and supporting each other in the search for personal value and wholeness which can be discovered outside the conventional sex roles." What they sought to achieve in these rap groups, Salutin wrote, was "a heightened awareness of ourselves, of each other and of men as they really are, as persons, rather than as objects for any kind of power play." Hunter published her phone number, too, so that interested women could call to find out how to get in on these "rap groups." In the end, Hunter concluded, "the struggle, finally, is individual. People must free themselves. If someone does it for them, all that has changed is the guard."

When I checked to see if these "rap groups" were forming in Surrey too, where women were arguably even more isolated within their "nuclear families," the closest thing I found was an organization for "single parents." They met every third Monday, presumably to discuss resources or to attempt to raise their own modest funds for worthy causes. They even held a dance one month, raking in over $200, which they donated to the Inter-section project. Did they see Inter-section as one of the few initiatives that might help them with the daunting task of raising their kids in this municipality with few resources?

The very existence of the single parents' organization suggested that "alternative family structures" were not unknown in Surrey — though it is unlikely that they were alternative by choice. And then in January 1974 the members came out of one of their meetings at a local school to find that their car tires had been slashed. They were pretty sure they had been specifically targeted, since other cars in the lot, at the school for a sports event, had been left unharmed. They reported it to the RCMP, hoping that something might be done to prevent further vandalism, but to no avail. The same thing happened at the next meeting. "Many of the people who attend these meetings ... are widows or divorcees who cannot afford the cost of replacing ruined tires," the article said, alerting me to the fact that it was mostly single female parents we were talking about here. One has to wonder, what was so threatening about women meeting to discuss their situation as single parents? It was especially troubling to think that some mysterious forces felt it necessary to discourage them from bringing their plight into the public sphere.

I questioned whether the women's movement had reached the "semi-rural" locale of Surrey. Oh, sure, there were a couple of women on the local Surrey council; and as was happening everywhere in North America, women had been entering the workforce in droves for some time now, though they still made only a fraction of the income of their male counterparts. I found a short filler on one of the pages of the *Surrey-Delta Messenger*, just titled "Smile" (as though ordering us to, whether we liked it or not), that conveyed the attitude toward working women in Surrey pretty succinctly: "A girl in an office explained why she had switched back from midis to minis: 'I've been in trouble ever since the boys started watching my work instead of my legs.'"

By '72 or '73 my own mother had forsaken her role as chief cook and bottle washer (not to mention chambermaid) at our motel for just such an office job as was depicted in this bit of nonsense about office "girls," at the same time that I was learning the art of "touch typing" in junior high. It was a mixed blessing, learning these clerical skills: on the one hand, it opened up a vista of something other than domestic chores in one's adult life; on the other hand, it was still belittled as "women's work."

Take Otto's tale of a bit of gender-bending he attempted in grade nine. He raised the ire of his father — and perhaps invited the derision of his peers — when he enrolled in a typing class as one of his electives. "My dad just about hit the roof," he said. "He just, oh my, 'What do you want to be, a secretary when you grow up?' He just couldn't stand this." But shortly after, as Otto's words-per-minute increased, his dad changed his tune. "You can type," he stated, with some enthusiasm now. "You're coming with me." And so every Monday night, both Ottos, Jr. and Sr., could be found at the council meetings, recording the relevant parts with their little cassette recorder. Then they'd go home, "and I'd have to type everything up," Otto said. "All of a sudden, typing was useful." Recording and typing were essential tools in the ongoing struggle against oppression. And Otto was now on the front lines.

The Whorehouse

"How come," one of my students asks, "almost every movie we've studied has prostitutes in it? What is it with the '70s and prostitution?"

This was in my "Scenes from the Seventies" film course. I'd proposed teaching it at about the same time I began researching my own youth, set in that same decade, with the intention to kill two birds with one stone — in this case, serve up an irresistible syllabus of fabulous '70s flicks and keep myself steeped in the imagery of the era I wished to mine for this book.

Why hadn't I noticed it myself? Jane Fonda as savvy call girl Bree Daniels, with her shag haircut and her bra-less midi-dress slouch, in the neo-noir *Klute*; Paula Kelly's prostitute-turned-spy in *The Spook Who Sat by the Door*; Diana Ross's fashion designer on the slippery slope to kept woman in *Mahogany*; Jodie Foster's wisecracking teen hooker in *Taxi Driver*. Even Faye Dunaway's television executive is really just the human stand-in for a "whorehouse Network" in Sidney Lumet's cynical lament about the pimping of hard news to make a corporate buck.

It must have something to do with the simultaneous rise of what Tom Burrows had referred to as "the whole women's lib thing," of course. If middle-class women were moving into the workforce in the '60s and '70s, and publicly demanding equal pay for their labour, popular culture reacted with its predictable symptoms — it was as though the term "working woman" or "professional woman" could not shed its nineteenth-century associations with prostitution. For what could women have, after all, that merited monetary compensation? It seemed impossible, as yet, to imagine a representation of a woman engaged in the public sphere that was not in one way or another tinged with harlotry.

The mudflats, too, had its "whorehouse" as I have mentioned, though it was no longer actively accommodating the trade it had been built for. Almost everyone I talked to told me about the whorehouse, as though it signified something intrinsic to the mudflats, something at the essence of what made them special. I first heard the tale from Paul Spong, who had been introduced to Peter Choquette, the hash dealer, who, in turn, offered to sell him this house that was, as Paul put it, "built way out on the boardwalk, sort of the furthest part of the mudflats, and I looked out and I thought 'fantastic'; I paid him six hundred bucks for it." He related the history of the house:

> *It originally came there because it was being used as a whorehouse, a brothel in, I think in False Creek, in Vancouver, and when that part of the city was cleared out by the authorities, it was towed out to the mudflats and somebody put it up on pilings. That's how my house came to be.*

So the whole thing was moved out to the mudflats from False Creek?

Well, Paul said,

> *It was one of these buildings that was on floats, like logs underneath it, so that it could be towed. Pretty simply. And it was, I have no idea when it was moved there, you know, when the city cleaned up False Creek, it was brought there. Sort of as a functioning structure that somebody obviously thought was good enough to take somewhere else. And they brought it up to the mudflats.*

For Ian Ridgway, what was remarkable about the whorehouse was its serendipitous role in the inauguration of the latest wave of squatters on the North Shore:

> *Originally there were several old guys who lived there, then a younger fella came along, and they told him, well, you're free to build yourself a little place there, 'cause they had all these piles of beautiful driftwood that kept coming into the little bay, so he was about ready to do that when a building floated in. And so he just decided to jack it up and*

build a boardwalk out to it and that would be his house. That was Peter Choquette. And his house eventually got taken over by Dr. Paul Spong.

Linda, too, shared this recollection that the house just sort of "drifted" in, as though under its own steam. She recalled it as a "cute little place" that had "floated up Burrard Inlet, and this guy, Peter Choquette, caught it, and he developed the mudflats." In her story the house was the first chapter in a development scheme, and in a sense this was true, insofar as Choquette charged the Spongs money for this "very cute little floathouse," and charged Tom Burrows, too, for the platform on which he built his house. According to Tom, the whorehouse had been situated among a cluster of squatted shacks just across Burrard Inlet from the Maplewood Mudflats:

> There was a bunch of shacks on the CPR [Canadian Pacific Railroad] property, there was a famous squatting community there. I guess the railway and the oil refinery got rid of these guys, and one of the shacks was actually a brothel, owned by this Hungarian guy, and it was very ornate, had all this gingerbread on it. It was an appealing-looking brothel. This was on the other side. It managed to make it across onto the mudflats.

So in Tom's story the whorehouse had already been in use by an earlier wave of squatters, though it may have had a previous history in the city, in some unspecified bygone era. That it travelled from one squatting community to another, or "managed to make it across onto the mudflats" as though by its own agency, was a reminder of how much of Vancouver's waterfront — whether it be Burrard Inlet, False Creek, Coal Harbour, or farther south along the Fraser River — was at one time or another inhabited by squatters living in boats, floathouses, cottages on pilings with water lapping at the floorboards, or simply shacks just up past the high-tide line. It wasn't only people who were transients along the watery edges of the city, but the very buildings themselves, either demolished and then reconstituted, board by window frame by newel post, in a makeshift neighbourhood, or drifting wholesale through the city's many waterways from one anchorage to another. You could fashion your place out of all the "beautiful driftwood" that just floated in, or if you were lucky you could latch onto a house as it drifted by.

As though she suspected I might doubt this legend that the floathouse had once been a bordello, Linda shrugged, offering what she thought might count as evidence: "It could have been a whorehouse. I mean, it was charming enough to be one." Its having been a brothel "sort of added to it," she said. And then, as though imitating her twenty-three-year-old self, "Really! We're living in a whorehouse! Wonderful!"

I gathered from this that it was not simply that the house had been a whorehouse that made it appealing, but that it had been a whorehouse in an earlier era — during the chapter of Vancouver's colonial history, perhaps, what with all that gingerbread, an ornateness that bespoke old-timey Victorian architecture, and old-timey sex roles where the men were prospectors and the women were scarlet. The very word "whorehouse" was meant to evoke the past. It was both architecturally and functionally quaint, as though drifting in not only from an elsewhere, but from the past itself, bringing with it a nostalgia for that earlier time — a nostalgia that had something to do with a fantasy of what life in the bawdyhouse must have been like when Vancouver was a frontier town.

The movie from the '70s that best exemplifies this droll version of the bordello is Robert Altman's *McCabe & Mrs. Miller*, a kind of muddy anti-western in which Warren Beatty's inept gambler falls for Julie Christie's business-minded madam in a rainy mountain mining town. The most distinct impression I had after seeing this film for the first time, long after its release in the early '70s, was of having wandered for hours through a drizzle or a torrent that turned into wet snowflakes, then back to rain again, and finally being buried — as McCabe is at the end — in mounds of muffling snowdrifts. As though I were revisiting, once again, the climate of my teen years. This impression was suffused with the creak of leather, drifting cigar smoke, the aroma of wet wool, like my dog's matted fur, and the plangent ballads of Leonard Cohen holding it all together. "It's true that all the men you knew were dealers/who said they were through with dealing/every time you gave them shelter" go the lyrics. This is McCabe's song; it floats him into the movie along with the opening credits, his face obscured in his big fur coat as the rain slicks through the fir trees. Maybe it's Mrs. Miller who's being addressed by this song, since it would seem to be McCabe who is the travelling stranger. But in her song, she too is the transient, a "Tra-a-velling Lady" asked to "stay awhile/until the night is over." Everyone's moving along in this movie, until they land in Presbyterian Church — the ironic place name given to a settlement where the chapel is only half built and nobody seems interested in worshipping anything but whisky and gold. In one scene, McCabe stumbles up to a makeshift wooden shack in the night and knocks on the door, hoping that Mrs. Miller will let him in. "I'm just a station on your way/I know I'm not your lover," Leonard Cohen sings. People sleep together in this movie, and they may even fall in love, but the ballads keep reminding us of the impermanence of all that, the brevity of intimacies.

On my second and third screenings, years later, it was the natural and half-built landscape for these characters that drew my eye — the wooden houses gradually taking shape in this mountain mining town, the backdrop of fir and pine across distant mountain passes, the boardwalks leading everywhere and nowhere. I don't remember when I intuited that the film was set in some coastal terrain near Vancouver, but I was not surprised when an article I read confirmed for me that Altman had come up to British Columbia to scout out this location, and that he spent weeks there, shooting the film in sequence, slowly documenting the construction of the village in a shallow valley littered with recently mined rubble, felled trees, scrap lumber, dirty canvas tents, and smoking cook fires. It is out of this muddy detritus that the cinematic whorehouse of all whorehouses takes shape, so that halfway through the film, when the high-class prostitutes themselves slog through pissing rain up into the village, they are greeted by Julie Christie as she leans over the deck-railing of an almost completed two-storey mansion of a bordello, its fresh lumber gleaming through the mist. This was Altman's distillation, his manifestation, of the '70s fantasy of the frontier pleasure-house, its interior rapidly filling up for us with the trappings of civilization, room by warmly lit room — the furnishings arriving by mail order and being set in motion, like the tall hand-cranked music box in the parlour that accompanies some sociable dancing before clients are led up to the bedrooms for business. If watching this film made me nostalgic — and it did — it was not turn-of-the-century lamplight and fiddle music that I longed for, but the milieu of my early teen years, when I ransacked the St. Vincent de Paul thrift shop for old-fashioned granny dresses and black orthopedic shoes that resembled Victorian ladies' boots. It was not so much an Edwardian colonial outpost that Altman's film evoked as Vancouver's recycling of itself as a squatters' village, its youth-culture homage to a pre-modern era. At one point a strange steam contraption chuffs and whistles its way slowly up into the village, a real vintage engine, which later pumps the water that will douse a fire engulfing the town's unfinished church. In retrospect, for a Vancouver audience, this steam engine does not so much hearken back to the emerging technology of the turn of the century as it anticipates the installation, a few years after the film's release, of a replica steam clock that was to dominate Vancouver's newly refurbished tourist quarter, Gastown, with its freshly renovated cobblestones, and its boutiques selling old-fashioned paraphernalia.

The famous environment of *McCabe & Mrs. Miller* was due to the artistic genius of production designer Leon Ericksen; he and Altman, it seems, were conducting a kind of cinematic experiment, shooting the film in sequence as the set was constructed.

> *The town — all raw wood, foot-deep mud, and piles of manure that steamed in the freezing winter air — was created by carpenters who lived in the cabins they were building and got drunk at night on whisky from the still they had also built ... The town grew as the script grew. Lots of things in the town changed because of the script; lots of things in the script changed because of the way the town was built. Everything happened organically.*

'Muddy detritus' of Presbyterian Church, and that ladder on the roof again. McCabe & Mrs. Miller. Courtesy Photofest

It was a lesson in immersion, an inhabitation of an earlier period and of living in shacks while the more "civilized" structures were being built — everything in chaotic states of construction from beginning to end of the film. And the grandest building of all, of course, was the whorehouse. This was because as the precipitation drenched the mountain, as it does every winter, runoff forming streams forming rivers with their rushing eddies and their stagnant backwaters, and as the whisky slaked the thirst of the characters, the actors, the crew, the director (who could sling back more than anyone), the capital was flowing too, along with the bodily fluids deposited each night by the miners in the welcoming vessels that were the prostitutes of the film. A high-end bordello, it appeared, was key to quickening the circulatory system of prosperity.

It was not just the mud, the half-built ignored church, the filthy miners, and the incomprehensible soundtrack that led everyone to call this the quintessential anti-Western, but the frankness with which it treated sex for money, casting the whole enterprise as at once much more visceral than in the classic Western, and at the same time a quaint matter of shared bawdiness among friends, after the miners and the women get to know each other. The tide of cash that washes into the movie as Mrs. Miller applies her financial talents to McCabe's brothel ensures that everyone enjoys all the creature comforts — proper linens, steamy hot baths, pink-frosted birthday cakes with candles, upholstered furniture, frilly window dressings, and rugs swept with the latest carpet-cleaning device. Outside, the characters pick their way among torn-up tree roots, two-by-fours, icy puddles, and backdrops of rough clay where a new road has been dynamited; inside, flirtatious ladies of the night tease the simple-natured miners. Sex is in the air, but laced with whimsy and the promise of prosperity. Bric-a-brac abounds — chandeliers, newel posts, banisters leading up to the chambers of pleasure.

Chandeliers, newel posts, banisters. It was Willie Wilson who brought all this Victorian adornment up the mountain to fill Altman's cinematic bordello. According to Ian Ridgway, Ericksen and art director Philip Thomas

> came down to the mudflats and looked at the mudflats and said, aha, here's our Chinatown [situated in the muddiest sector of the film's town, the Chinese workers' shacks were built on stilts]. So they reproduced the mudflats authentically as the Chinatown, up the Cypress street side, and I and several others worked up there building things, during the show ... we built some things and then we weren't really acting in it, but sometimes they were shooting stuff while we were building 'cause that was part of the story of how things got built.

If there was a mudflats aesthetic in *McCabe & Mrs. Miller*, it was because Altman's team found a way to recreate the world of the mudflats up in the mountains just a few miles away. It was the mudflats squatters who were living in the cabins they built up there, and who appeared in the background of some shots. Ridgway and his construction partner, mudflats squatter Dan Clemens, with their experience building old-timey Pleasure Faires for years, used a combination of salvaged wood and the endless Victorian bric-a-brac that Willie Wilson had hauled over the inlet from all the Vancouver building stock that was being torn down.

Ridgway and Clemens had also built, or elaborated on, many of the complex and rambling shacks that defined the mudflats' distinct architectural panache. It was this "look," as well as the process of how that look was achieved, that Altman's artistic team brought into the organic enterprise that was the making of his film: Altman "was coming up here and he wanted this thing to look very authentic," Ridgway said, "and so he deliberately got all these hairy people to build all these cabins and then the idea was to come in and film them all and there they would actually be, very authentic looking, because there they were." Ridgway worked on the second set as well, in Squamish, a waterfront town an hour north of the mudflats, on the tip of Howe Sound, which was meant to represent a more bustling settlement where McCabe buys his first trio of prostitutes.

"It was a little more than just making a movie," Ridgway said. "It was also a time of spiritual awakening. These guys were into meditation and, you know, really eating well, and very organically, and had a bit of a higher aim than just this movie thing." It was a sort of "encounter group," as Dan Clemens put it, but also a bunch of people having fun with Hollywood money until the producers put an end to it all. I had read the stories about the community ethos, the experiment in living, the voracious drinking, and rumours of an illegal still in books and news bits about Altman's filmmaking style. But what was becoming clear to me now was that in the case of this Altman film in particular, it was these squatters, their aesthetic, their ethic, their laid-back lifestyle, their reincarnation of Vancouver's beginnings on a fringe landscape, connected by wooden boardwalks, and, most of all, the ubiquity of mud that defined the essence of Altman's cinematic experience this time — for the participants in the creation of the movie illusion, and just as much for the audience. You could take a cynical view of this, of course, as did Vancouver art critic Scott Watson, the first writer I came upon to have publicly linked the Altman set to the mudflats:

Mudflat Dreaming

As the sets were being built up the mountain, a hippie "Pleasure Faire" was being constructed on the flats: another ersatz village that mirrored the one for the movie that in turn mirrored the squat itself. The movie and the Pleasure Faire showed that the authentic squatter's shack could be reproduced and circulated by the image industry and was also a ready-made commodity fetish for the emerging hippie entrepreneurial reinvestment of drug money.

'So they reproduced the mudflats authentically as the Chinatown.'
McCabe & Mrs. Miller. Courtesy Photofest

To an extent, this endless simulation of the past in the present — of the mudflats on the movie set, the squatter's shack as "commodity fetish," the recycled rags and feathers of the Victorian era turning up as the countercultural dress code — does invite a jaundiced glance. But Scott Watson did not quite get at the melancholy sense of doom that pervaded it all, thus providing it with its attraction. The absence of a happy ending is the other thing that makes *McCabe & Mrs. Miller* the exception to the rule of the classic Western: the corporate powers that threaten the individuals of the film, what in '70s parlance would have been known as "The Establishment," seem somehow to have turned all the rain to an impossibly heavy blizzard. In the final scene, shot over two days, but whose fictional duration could not be more than an hour, the snow piles up to holster-high drifts, bringing the dying hero to a complete stasis by seeming to cement him over, like so much hardening concrete. The fire that burns the half-finished church is extinguished by the others; this village will not be bulldozed or burned out, but steamrollered in another way by corporate developers. In one of the mudflats documentaries, an abashed worker, whose bulldozer has been temporarily stalled by Paul Spong and his fellow squatters, shakes his head and smiles sadly: "You canna stop p-r-r-rogress," he says in his Scots burr.

But what of the whorehouse? I had turned to *McCabe & Mrs. Miller* because of its cinematic mirroring of the pioneer bordello down on the flats. If Altman's movie, as Scott Watson put it, was "a frontier parable in which hippie ideals played out against the long arm of speculative interests," then what did prostitution have to do with it?

I conjure up the image, once more, of a high-angle long shot of Altman's mining village, slashed into the mountainside, the mix of ramshackle huts and newly constructed saloons, barbershop, bordello scattered about amid logging detritus: limbs, trunks, upended roots, recently excavated stumps, and water running freely in every direction, unimpeded by foliage, causing mucky erosions. Evidence, too, of mining activity, since this is a mining town, where zinc is hauled out of holes in the nearby mountainside, leaving piles of tailings everywhere. This is the film's allusion to what was already defining British Columbia at the turn of the twentieth century: an enthusiastic willingness to extract as many resources as possible — timber, zinc, copper, gold, coal, salmon — and send them on their way to foreign lands. The scarred hillside of Altman's film is a suggestive reference to huge swathes of devastation on almost every accessible mountain along the coast or up the rivers into the interior of BC. The free-flowing rains rushing along the movie's sodden ground are a vague allusion to the hundreds of thousands of old-growth trees severed at the base, stripped of their branches, and sent down the river or, where there was no river, down endless wooden flumes to the waterways in the lowlands, to be corralled in log booms and pulled out toward the sawmills, the ships, the railyards. If Vancouver were to become the city of international renown that it wished to be, it had to define itself as the most efficient thoroughfare for the export of natural resources that Canada had to offer, the place where no time was lost getting the lumber, the ore, the coal, the rapidly canned salmon out to the rest of the world. Every waterway became a flume in its own right for the massive exportation of the forests, the earth's elements, and, soon enough, fossil fuel. The province would strip itself of its plenty, and the city would be the well-greased point of transfer to the outside world. Along the waterfront, then, there came railways linking west to east, north to south, and once the surrounding valleys and the Fraser River delta had been deforested, drained, and solidified with the aid of dykes and dams, highways were built to accommodate the ubiquitous mammoth logging trucks: the Trans-Canada Highway, the Sea to Sky Highway, the King George Highway. What had Vancouver made of itself but a giant whorehouse, pimping the province's riches to the highest bidder.

Sisters of Mercy

A third song weaves through *McCabe & Mrs. Miller* — a gentle waltz, sung by Cohen as though in tribute to the prostitutes of the film, those "Sisters of Mercy" who were "waiting for me when I thought/that I just can't go on." The conceit, of course, is that the women of the northwest night, whose address can be read "by the moon," bring a kind of salvation to the lonely wanderer if they touch both his eyes, and he touches the "dew on their hem." This is all part of a ritual of absolution, the unexpected feminine forgiveness for a wilderness of drifting, drinking, gambling. As a spectator of the film, I'm addressed by Cohen's lyrics directly when he invokes a "you" in his song: "I hope you run into them," he sings, "you who've been travelling so long." Because Cohen and the film want to share something with me, something that will comfort me even though my loneliness tells me I've sinned.

Visually, the prostitutes may seem comic at first, awkward, too young, dressed in the drab rags of poverty when McCabe purchases them for a pittance in Bearpaw. Relegated to makeshift tents where they crudely ply a trade that we must assume they have only just learned, their only purpose, at that point, is to demonstrate his inexperience in the sex trade business. Even the more "high-class" ladies that Mrs. Miller brings later are drenched and bedraggled when they first trudge up into the village, swearing and sneering, through a classic northwest downpour. But Cohen's lyrics, and then a communal baptismal scene, turn these unkempt harpies into good-natured objects of desire — and human "characters" in their own right, each with her own personality.

Let's go back to that moment when Julie Christie leans out from the upper deck of the grand new whorehouse that has replaced the sorry pup-tents down in the mud. "Thought you'd like to look at my beautiful ladies," she mutters, motioning to Lily, one of the three "chippies" hired by McCabe in Bearpaw, and pointing out into the rain. "Give them a hot bath, go on," she orders, thus marking Lily's transition from prostitute to domestic employee. Mechanical wheels are turned, steaming water flows through a network of wooden flumes, and next thing we see is an intimate shot of the women joking and soaking in two expansive cedar tubs. The camera cuts to the saloon, where the miners play poker around a table, spinning out naïve fantasies about the women, then cuts back again to the women, luxuriating in their bond of community in the bathhouse. The homoeroticism among the new prostitutes would only come across as hetero soft porn if it weren't for a final point-of-view shot that invites me in too: as the women's banter shades off into a lilting rendition of "The Daring Young Man on the Flying Trapeze," the camera cuts away from their steam-caressed bodies, swaying in harmony, to a close-up of Lily's face as she takes in the scene, rapt, mesmerized, desiring. This is the last gaze of the scene, a counter-shot to the men's foolish commentary. Lily is awed by these women's apparent worldliness, but is also a part of their world now. As the fire nearby keeps the bathwater warm, its golden flicker kindles her look, relays it to my own.

The question was, what position could I have taken in this hippie world of hetero free love, where lesbian desire was still merely an uncertain innuendo? Mrs. Miller was yet another prostitute on the Hollywood screen, but she was also meant to resonate with women's lib, given her hard head for money matters and her facilitation, or so it would seem, of a strong women's community in a man's world — albeit a community whose *raison d'être* was to comfort the lowly miner. Could homoeroticism and intimacy among women be only a side effect, salvaged as the waste product of the central commodity of hetero transactions? Is it me Cohen's song addresses with his story of the Sisters of Mercy?

'I'm a cook'

If I've been able to find the mudflats carpenters who helped construct the famous set of *McCabe & Mrs. Miller*, I wonder, might I also be able to track down at least one of the bit players who populated the village of show business people who came together to participate in Altman's cinematic experiment? I pore over the list of minor cast members, looking up this one and that, until I hit the jackpot in the person of Jackie Crossland, who played none other than the prostitute-turned-cook Lily. Turns out Jackie spent a lifetime on the activist side of show business; her gig with Altman was just a brief moment in an illustrious career as an actress, playwright, director, and theatre arts administrator — most of it spent in Vancouver. Moreover, she had become something of a celebrity in the city's queer arts and theatre scene. One of the web pages I discovered was of a brief 2007 interview with her and her partner, Nora Randall: a compilation of reminiscences about Vancouver's

Commercial Drive back in the day, as it was turning into a mecca for lesbian culture.

We agreed to meet at Rhizome Café, on Broadway near Main Street — where a couple of weeks later I returned to attend a roundtable about media treatment of Occupy Vancouver (the local version of Occupy Wall Street, which had snowballed into a broad social movement protesting income and wealth inequality, and calling for social and economic justice and new forms of democracy). Rhizome seemed a fitting place for our rendezvous — almost a twenty-first-century Cecil Hotel, but with a much more palpably diverse clientele if you considered its ownership by two women and the hundreds of events it hosted, ranging from Queer Cuban Salsa classes, to an educational session on fair trade, from a forum on the Venezuelan revolution to speakers on the threat of for-profit medical clinics to Canada's Medicare system, from a night of hip hop in commemoration of the Sikh genocide in 1984 to a reading by Ivan Coyote, one of my favourite Vancouver queer storytellers.

I recognized Jackie right away despite her salt-and-pepper short hair, silver tufts framing her broad forehead. She had that same open-mouthed smile, the same weather-reddened round cheeks, the same stock-taking glint in her eye — or maybe it was just amusement about my wanting to interview her.

We swapped stories about our shared alma mater, Simon Fraser University, though she started there only two years after it opened in 1965, whereas I didn't arrive until '75, eight years later. Jackie was one of the slightly older students SFU catered to, already in her mid-twenties when she enrolled after a hard-scrabble youth: high-school dropout in Port Arthur, Ontario; married at a young age; came with her husband out to Vancouver in search of work, expecting to transplant to California. But between the two of them they were just getting by, her husband in construction, Jackie as a housemaid in West Van. "Twelve hours a day, five days a week, and Saturday if they wanted me, you know. It was rugged. And I think the pay was $75 a month."

Except for the prostitute part, her life story was sort of meshing

Jackie Crossland as Lily (far right). Also shown (l to r): Warren Beatty, Elizabeth Murphy, Carey Lee McKenzie. **McCabe & Mrs. Miller.** Courtesy Photofest

in my mind with the character she played in *McCabe*, or, rather, with what I imagined her character's backstory to be. For instance, she told this story of that time: it was the late '60s, her life wasn't going anywhere, and she noticed "that the salespersons in the Hudson's Bay Department store were the most beautiful women I'd ever seen."

> I was totally in love with them, not having a clue what this meant. And I used to, on Saturdays, go up and down the escalator at the Hudson's Bay, just to look at them. And they were dressed in classy black dresses, and accessorized, and seemed so very, very beautiful.

Was she consciously rhyming this scene with Lily in the movie, gazing her fill of Julie Christie's "beautiful ladies?" I hadn't even asked her about that scene yet.

Whether she wanted to be these ladies or have them, it didn't matter — she was spurred on to get her high-school equivalency, going to night classes. "I'd been working since I was about thirteen," she said, so it was about time she finished school. At community college she was encouraged to go to SFU, where she found herself among a "hotbed of American radicals who had come up from the war," and became a "foot soldier" in the anti-war movement while making her way toward an English degree. She had upgraded her goal from salesclerk to librarian, and it was the professors she worshipped now, people like Kathleen Aberle, Andrea Lebowitz, and Jerry Zaslove.

"That's where I discovered learning as an important piece of my life," she marvelled. "I realized I had never been happy before then. It was just the most wonderful place to be." As she gained confidence, her aspirations morphed again, and "having met the hippies and, you know, the dope culture, and the theatre ... it didn't take me long to be like a little campus mini-star, and then the writing was on the wall." She laughed. "I was no longer going to library school."

"No library school for you." I laughed with her.

"No, no, no." She wiped her eyes. "'Cause you can't wear red velvet there, can you? And I had a big yen to wear flashy clothes."

Although she found herself doing housework again after graduation, she could now think of it as her "day job," allowing her to make ends meet while she plunged deep into the theatre world. She and her peers were all thinking through the longer-term options for a "young actor with tremendous potential." If you went south, you'd be doing the movies. If you wanted legitimate theatre, you had to go back east — Stratford, the Shaw Festival at Niagara-on-the-Lake, Quebec. You could learn the mid-Atlantic accent and maybe get some work in the UK. But it all seemed "so far away, and there was nothing that was really reflecting Canadian experience at all." She could hook up with British radical theatre, she said, "but as an artist, you need your own context. You need what you're grounded in. So we came to the conclusion that we would just have to make our own theatre."

And that she did. By '72 she had written, published, and produced her own play and was, like others, trying to snag some of the government grants that were starting to become available.

"So when *McCabe* turned up in town, there were quite a large number of people fighting to make Canadian culture." There were three movies "in town" at that time, Jackie recalled. Altman's, Mike Nichols's *Carnal Knowledge*, and a third she'd forgotten. "Everyone thought it was the beginning of the revolution or something," she said. "We hadn't drawn that kind of attention before. It was kind of the beginning of the movie industry on the West Coast."

"Hollywood North?" I chimed in.

"Yeah, that didn't really happen until the '80s, but it was kinda there."

Jackie was living in the West End with her husband in "one of these huge old houses that got cut up into suites in the post-war ... this was just the beginning of the development boom, '68 sort of saw that in." She remembered a building going up nearby. "We were all agog at the size of the hole they dug in the ground and how high it went up."

So how did she get involved with *McCabe*? Well, she said, she and her friends were all "hustling our buns to keep working," and they heard Altman liked to work with Canadian actors, as he had done a couple of years before when he shot *That Cold Day in the Park* with Sandy Dennis in Vancouver.

So would he go around and watch local theatre productions? "Might have done," Jackie said vaguely. "But he was sleeping with somebody I knew also."

"So you had a connection?"

"Well, yeah, but we all did ... this [person Altman was sleeping with] wasn't a person that nobody knew, so we heard everything. Never were so many ears to the ground for opportunities. We were all making theatre day and night, we were all extremely competitive." Altman asked someone "who should I audition," and Jackie's name came up. "By then I'd worked up a bit of a rep, so I wasn't kind of a local nobody.

"We must have just been insufferably arrogant," Jackie recalled, because they'd recite this "huge bullshit line about, 'well, I don't know if I can really do that'" (i.e. forsake theatre for the movies, I assumed). She laughed the line down, "Yes you can, yes you can, and you will!"

After all, apart from the exciting concept Altman had for the film, it also meant three months of steady work, being on the set all the time, soaking it all up. "We were like sponges, you know."

The situation was unlike most film sets in that the bit players would be paid to stay on the set at all times, not only on days when they were in a scene.

> *You didn't work every day, but you had to be kind of on the ball every day, 'cause you might be called. So you couldn't leave the mountain. Somebody used to pick me up really early in the morning, whatever my makeup call was, and then we'd be back home at night.*

They hung out in the trailers just off the set, sitting in on an ongoing poker game, or "for a while there was a pick-up stix tournament. I was Rene Auberjonois's partner at pick-up stix." You couldn't mess with the half-built village except when you might be on set for a scene.

In conversation with the bit players, the hookers in particular, Altman would encourage them to develop scenarios. He could "lead you down a lot of paths," Jackie said.

> *So we had conversations about who that person was, and there were situations where although it was a film and you had to meet your marks and all, there was opportunity to do quite a lot of improvisation. You were deliberately put into scenes that you weren't written into, because the idea was to have the life in the town go on as it would go on, in the background, and sometimes he would like some of what he saw and he would pull it and use it. He would develop that storyline, and there'd be lines or a new scene for somebody. It was the best possible way to start working in film because you were actually doing creative work.*

If some people thought it was "kind of flakey," or they "wanted more structure," for Jackie it was a place where "things could happen." The half-built town was "an environment where I think life could take place, you could fill that up."

I asked about Jackie's role as Lily, what about her scenes? Well, she said, Altman knew they were all primarily theatre people, he liked that. And so "you got attention for being a good improviser, and I was pretty good, I think. There were a lot of storylines developed with me and John Schuck," who played Smalley, one of the prominent townsmen, who opens the movie with humorous advice to a miner about the cut of his facial hair.

"There was a kind of love story that evolved" between Lily and Smalley, Jackie recalled. "But it never got into the film. Everybody had three or four of those backstories."

I was getting excited now, thinking, This makes sense! Lily wouldn't have a backstory with a male character; she's got her eye on the "beautiful ladies" that have come to town.

I finally told Jackie my reading of that steaming bath scene, Lily's gaze hinting at a lesbian subtext. But she dashed my fantasy: "The only direction I would have received for that was something on the order of, these are the new people in town, and does that mean you might soon be out of a job? Nasty as that job was?"

I still clung to my read of the scene, though. After all, in leaving out the hetero love story with Smalley, didn't Altman allow for my lesbian subtext? But now we were interrupted by the arrival of Nora, Jackie's partner of twenty-three years. I could have sworn she said "you forgot your hobo," and now I can't recall what it was she brought to Jackie. Was it a walking stick? I was preoccupied, I guess, with the impression that her true motive in showing up at Rhizome was to check me out. Who was this American academic coming to interview her Jackie? I passed muster, apparently, as they exchanged a few words and then Nora took off again.

Then Jackie recalled a moment in the film that she may have been responsible for improvising, when Lily is approached by one of the miners in the general hubbub of the brothel, and she stops him cold.

"'I'm not a whore anymore, I'm a cook,' she says. They left that in the film. 'I'm a cook!'"

It seems like a little throwaway line, but it was an important touch-point in the film — if not for Jackie so much, then for someone she met who quoted it back to her years after the fact. "I worked for a while with street kids, juvenile prostitutes in downtown Vancouver," she remembered, "and somebody I worked with, the minute he met me he recognized me from that movie. In the job interview he said, 'Are you in a movie?' and what he remembered was this line I had, 'I'm not a whore anymore, I'm a cook.'"

So prostitution was not just a cinematic fiction in this scenario, but a part of the daily life Jackie had entered. I don't know if this guy who associated Jackie with this line he had so loved was a potential co-worker being interviewed for his job or one of the street kids being interviewed for something other than sex work — that's what this job involved, Jackie said, getting jobs for the kids.

She had at first worked in a street contact program, hired to "do theatre with the street kids," but after a while that seemed to be a dead end, "for the kids as well as for me." She didn't like the politics of it:

> *In some ways the kids liked the experience of it and all that, but it led them to huge false expectations; when things were over, life was kind of crap. I think everybody in the project kind of realized what they needed was a job, what they want is work, so maybe if we bent our collective efforts towards that, that would be a more useful and more realistic thing.*

There's always a "false glamour around theatre." So into her work with streetwise juvenile prostitutes, Jackie brought this little bit of glamour, having played a prostitute herself and, okay, it's a funny line — as with most of Altman's characters, you're laughing both with her and at her.

I'm thinking about another moment in the film now, a birthday party, where Lily, in her role as cook, has just decorated a cake with pink frosting. She's hesitantly proud of her work, glancing shyly at Mrs. Miller for approval. But she has as much frosting on her face as on the cake. She's a novice cook, but she's a cook now, see, not a whore. This is what the street kid saw, or maybe her co-worker, this little flash of aspiration to become something else.

And speaking of becoming something else, I wondered about

how Jackie made the transition from married woman to queer theatre activist. When did she come out? What was the gay and lesbian scene like in the early '70s in Vancouver? Did she have a sense of who she might be becoming in '71 or '72?

Not exactly, she said, but all through the '60s and early '70s she was well aware of "the sort of polymorphous perverse thing ... anybody with anybody is possible, so I kind of maybe put myself there a little bit." In '73 she went to Toronto for four years, and while she was separated from her husband "the marriage kind of fizzled." Or as she put it, "When I left Vancouver, I was sort of still thinking of myself as this married woman, but after four years I realized that that was ridiculous. This wasn't an extended shopping trip. My life was my own." They separated but never divorced, and by the time her husband died, in 1986, "I was identified to myself as a lesbian."

She recalled an interview with a friend in a local gay paper: "She was asked about coming out, and she said, I don't think I really came out, I think I oozed out, and when I read that I just loved it. That's what sort of happened to me."

I wanted to bring the conversation back to the mudflats. I knew Jackie was living in one of those big old West End houses, but had she or any of her fellow actors ever lived among the squatters, on the beach in North Van District? It turned out to be a naïve question, because, as Jackie put it, theatre people "were more involved with telephones. I mean, you would need to be able to take calls." Like, for acting gigs. So you'd need an address and a phone number if you wanted to be reached. But she did go down there once or twice, she said. To visit a woman who lived on a barge, an artist, Jackie thought, "and I know she tried to keep it going for a long time, and then eventually she got froze out one winter, the thing was falling apart, it was too damned old, so she just moved into town with friends." No glamour there.

And what about the Pleasure Faires, had she gone to any of those? Oh yeah, she said, she remembered driving for an hour and a half to this field in the Fraser Valley somewhere. "And you know, it was all very wonderful, and then the people that I was with didn't want to go home when I wanted to go home, and it started to get heavy. You know, the band started getting heavier, it was getting to be a bit of an edgier scene, and I wanted to go home."

"Edgier as in druggier?"

"Yeah, a little more nervous-making. I mean, I did my share of party drugs, but it wasn't just somebody smoking a joint ... I think maybe something set me off and made me a bit paranoid. I was scared!"

Not wanting to be a drag on her friends, she walked out to a payphone to call someone to come get her.

"Part of the rules then was, you could go, but you couldn't make it heavy for someone else."

"Saying you wanted to go home was making it heavy?"

"Yeah." She seemed slightly apologetic for not daring to break this unspoken rule. "Unless you found somebody in the same space, you couldn't do much," she mused. "And I was sort of way too much into people-pleasing."

So that seemed to be the two choices for a woman who wasn't feeling the "pleasure" of the Pleasure Faire: making it heavy for someone else, or being a people-pleaser. You couldn't win, it seemed.

We talked about the Occupy movement in Vancouver, and about the dire housing situation in the city today. She said she understood the movement in Wall Street, but in Vancouver it seemed destined to peter out. "I mean, this huge imperial country, it's not gonna go down easy," she said. In the '60s and '70s, "we knew what we were doing at those demos. And I think people just have this overwhelming feeling that things are just wrong now, but what they want to replace that with is not so clear." Even so, "I think it's pretty important to do these things." She herself would have joined the Occupy encampment at the Vancouver Art Gallery if she were a young person today. "It goes back to Jean-Paul Sartre's saying: 'It's not necessary to hope in order to act, but sometimes it's just necessary to act.'"

Helen Simpson

After talking to Jackie, I wondered about that woman on the barge she visited. Who was she? No one else had mentioned her in their stories. But there was a woman who sort of fit this description, though she was not frozen out of a barge she was living on. I associated her, somehow, with that most famous of all Leonard Cohen songs about Suzanne who takes you down, who gets you on her wavelength and lets the river answer that you've always been her lover.

I've already mentioned her, in passing: the sun-bronzed beauty seen stringing beads in one of the films, who tells us about her dance of survival after she left the world of payrolls and welfare rolls. The movie does not name her and seems more interested in gliding along her golden, bead- and silver-adorned limbs than in exploring the question of how she survives — surely it's not just by selling that jewellery she's making.

This was Helen Simpson, Linda told me — a woman who lived on her own in one of the cabins, a longtime friend of the same Peter Choquette who had sold the Spongs their first shack. "Maybe she sold drugs," Linda mused, then took it back. "I don't know how she survived."

It is Helen's voice that comments on the environmental value of the mudflats at the film's end, and it's Helen who has a despairing confrontation with the officials who show up to mow down their shacks. The camera circles around behind her to reveal a city official standing sheepishly near a yellow bulldozer. Helen clutches a patterned serape around her shoulders, her rain-dampened hair matted to the back of her head.

"Man, lookit, man, yer gonna cover that with cement, man?" She points offscreen, her face distorted. "S'part of yer job," she jeers. "That's my home there." She sobs on the word "home," like someone has just slugged her. "That's where I belong. I belong in this area. I've lived here all my life. You're gonna do that to my house?"

"I'm not doing it," retorts the city official, offended by all this snivelling incivility.

'I've lived here all my life!' Helen Simpson confronts the bulldozers.
Livin' On the Mud, Sean Malone and Ed Dupras

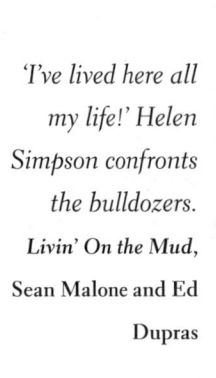

"You are so," Helen shrieks, no longer able to contain herself. "You're doing it, youuuu're doing it, you and you." She sniffs. "And him, and him."

It's a different season now, the season of raw frustration, of rage. I was embarrassed for Helen; didn't she know that yelling wouldn't get her anywhere? Shouldn't she have been using clever speeches, subtle irony? Don't show how much pain you are in, I want to say. They don't give a shit.

Is that why the filmmakers never flashed an identifying name across the screen when Helen appeared? To make her an anonymous victim? Audiences would know who Paul Spong was, and Tom Burrows and Mayor Ron Andrews. But not Helen.

I was surprised, then, when it turned out that Helen was a bit of a celebrity around Vancouver. Before she moved to the mudflats, she was what Dan Clemens called one of the city's more prominent beatniks in the '60s.

Beatnik? I hadn't thought of the mudflats crowd as having a beatnik provenance; it seemed more of a hippie scene.

Oh yeah, Dan said, "You know the classic look of the black leotards and the long black hair? Helen would have been the grand dame of that. It would have been her they took the photographs of."

When I contacted Dan, Helen Simpson was the first person he wanted to talk about. I'd heard from others that she had died young, from cancer, just a few years after the squatters had been chased off the flats. But no one offered any more than a few vague words here or there. Dan, though, was insistent that I get a full portrait of Helen. She was a sort of hero for him.

> First, there was her intensity. She was a beautiful woman, very striking, but what she really was, was intense, and nobody ever had a casual conversation, no one got away with sort of loose talk about these big issues ... she thought that her job was to call our bullshit on most of it, you know.

"'Are you in or are you out?'" Dan remembered her insistence. "And we'd say, 'We're in, we're in!' She had a very piercing way of pulling people in." She was the first environmentalist Dan had met, a stance that grew out of the close attention she had paid over the years to what was happening on the north shore of Burrard Inlet, all the way from the First Narrows (at the mouth of the inlet) to the mudflats — the landfill, the development, the industry. She didn't have the patience "to do all those meetings the Greenpeace people did. You know, the NGO-type thing, sitting around just smoking cigarettes and talking." Her thing was more action, living on the mudflats and working to keep that last little bit of North Vancouver from being paved over. She had a little saying, Dan said, "North Shore, foreshore, for sure." He laughed. Something like that.

Helen was a singer and songwriter, he said, and I found a song she had written about the mudflats in a dog-eared copy of a fringe publication Dan turned me on to, *West Coast Song Book* — a collection of folk and Fraser Valley–style country songs by Vancouver artists from the '60s and '70s, some of whose names (like Shari Ulrich and Doug and the Slugs) I had not heard for forty years. Helen's lyrics covered all the aspects of the flats I'd read about before, the "big flame" of the "refinery 'cross the bay," the rhythm when "tides flow in and tides flow out," the "bird-pecked grass and mud-trapped tide." Rain splashes through her house and "out the floor," while she hangs on the "edge of time," her mind sliding "through the door of space inside alone." It didn't really make sense, but I was struck by the solitary aura around this singer in her rain-sluiced house, "inside alone." No score was provided, so I had no idea how the tune went. But Helen would have sung it, accompanied by her guitar.

"She never wasn't writing, she was always writing," Dan said. "I don't think she published anything, but ... I think that she would introduce herself to you as a poet. That's how she spoke and talked, and she was very much a wordsmith, and read everything that ever came near her and all that kind of stuff, she was really the real deal."

Always that fragility of the manuscript written on the mudflats, as in the Lowry legends, where the half-burned pages of *Under the Volcano* were rescued from the charred remains of Lowry's shack on the beach. But in this case, hardly a trace was found of this woman who wrote and wrote, sang, and fought the good fight. According to Dan,

> She almost ... she wasn't a gay woman or anything, but she was very much a dominant, always the dominant player in a relationship. She got boyfriends, boyfriends didn't get her type of thing. She looked like a man in that way, you know. She had a variety of handsome young men suit her, but she, she was the old sage.

By "old sage," Dan meant that Helen was in her wise old thirties, and from the naïve vantage point of her twenty-something fellow squatters she seemed already to possess a world of experience. Was he trying to say that her authority in the erotic department came from her slight edge in maturity over the rest of them? She didn't literally "look" like a man, of course; it was her behaviour that was like a man's — that forthright decision to choose whom she slept with, not to be chosen. And somehow this translated into travel to foreign places: if someone was going to "the Andes," for instance, "they would want Helen to come and share that experience and she would go down and do things like that." She had a "good eye," it seemed, for "all the things that were being bought in those days,

'Through the door of space inside alone.' Helen Simpson's house.
David Wisdom

the international weavings and all that." So maybe that, too, was how she performed the dance of survival — getting in on the craze for foreign imports and bringing back the kinds of exotic fare we'd find at Trident Imports, down in Gastown.

So it turned out that women's lib had, in some respect, made it to that semi-rural place down on the mudflats, in the person of Helen Simpson. "She was a strong female," Dan stated solemnly. "When women were just finding themselves, she was already there! No doubt about it."

Bridgeview Residents

In the film about Bridgeview, only a couple of the residents are named: Otto Wittenberg and Alice Wilcox. But we see others who are not identified: a gruff man at a convenience store counter who comments that a kindergartner could do a better job than those up at city council, who are just a bunch of . . .; a mother interviewed against a wood-panelled wall, family portraits arrayed on the shelf behind her, who promises, "If I have to get a shotgun, they won't phase me out"; a woman and her daughter laughing as they herd two white geese back into their yard.

I wanted to know more about who lived in Bridgeview. What else could Otto tell me about growing up there? And did he experience the stigma I had seen, in my own teen years, that was attached to that community "on the flats"?

"Of course there was a stigma," he said. "You must know it yourself. I mean, Whalley's got kind of a stigma."

He figured this was a shared legacy, this growing up with a stigma. He thought it over for a few seconds, then admitted that there were some "unsavoury" characters who lived near them — three families in particular whose kids would gang up on him and his little brother, "always causing trouble, you know. You'd get bullied, that kind of stuff." Most of the kids his age were "all at one time or another in jail. So, you know. Little hoods." He laughed, remembering another set of "unsavoury" characters, visitors who used to show up at their door when they first purchased their house. "Because they used to do bootlegging from that house," he explained. He meant the former owners. He told me his wife was laughing too, in the background. "I remember seeing some people I didn't recognize, whatever, and my mum was just totally, 'Don't look at them, don't talk to them' kind of an attitude."

This mention of "bootleggers," like the "whorehouse" on the Maplewood Mudflats, seemed like a remnant from a different era, superimposed somehow on the '70s. As though Vancouver's outlying edge settlements were still haunted by a once-upon-a-time: the colonial mining boom, the prohibition era, and, as I was about to learn, the Second World War.

Otto Jr. told me about Franz Stigler, another German immigrant, who became friends with his family during the ditch and sewer battles. Franz and his family lived in a house that afforded a view of the on-ramp of the Pattullo Bridge, with room enough in the backyard for "a small, aged grey horse named Lighty and a scary, hairy beast of a dog named Souchi," Otto recalled. I was put in mind of a glimpse we get in *Some People Have To Suffer* of three teens riding horses down one of the roads in Bridgeview; the neighbourhood was ahead of the curve where the "urban livestock" movement of today is concerned.

But there was so much more to know about Franz than his modest life in this urban-rural locale. "If you dig away the surface, most people actually have interesting lives," Otto said, "but Franz Stigler's story is fantastic." Otto alluded to a biography of Franz, titled *A Higher Call*, which told the story of his experience as a fighter pilot for the Luftwaffe during the Second World War. It turns out that Franz Stigler's story was so legendary as to inspire not just this book, but countless television reports across the globe, internet tributes, and even battle simulations in the digital gaming world.

Like the Wittenbergs, Franz Stigler immigrated to Canada some years after the war; he had worked as a mechanic in logging, mining, and sawmills, according to Otto, before settling with his family in Bridgeview. I tracked down a 1997 BCTV news report on Stigler, where he was interviewed in what must have been his Bridgeview home, a kind of shrine full of memorabilia and photos of Second World War fighter planes. He rummages in a treasure chest of medals and ribbons, then holds up one displaying the number "400." "For four hundred combat missions," Franz says sort of absent-mindedly, though the voiceover informs us that he actually flew close to five hundred.

Knowing his story now, I imagine him, back in the '70s, living with the secret that he had been carrying for over twenty years, and which he would harbour for another twenty. In 1943, just a few days before Christmas, Stigler was finishing up one of his routine sorties when he saw a lone American B-17 limping by, trailing smoke from the battle it had just barely survived. Stigler went back up and gave chase. When he caught up with the plane, he saw how severely it had been damaged, its nose practically blown off, and surmised that there were likely dead and injured inside.

"Had you ever seen a bomber so badly damaged?" asks the interviewer.

"Not flying," Stigler says, with some amazement.

Pulling up closer to the plane, Franz could see the tail-gunner just lying there, bleeding profusely. He should have pulled the trigger and finished off the enemy plane, but something in him hesitated.

"If I wouldn't have seen him ..." he says. "Well, it's different. If I wouldn't have seen a person at all, I would have shot."

"But they're the enemy," the interviewer urges.

"But you shoot at the airplane, you don't think of people in there. You see the airplane, a plane that bombs your cities or your factories or whatever, but in this case ... just ... couldn't do it."

Franz pulled up alongside the pilot instead and tried to signal to him that he should either land or fly to safety in Sweden. They continued to fly side by side, out over the North Sea, until Franz finally saluted goodbye and returned to his own base.

It wasn't an incident he could report to his fellow pilots, and certainly not to his superiors, since he "didn't want to look at the firing squad." So he kept silent about this forbidden encounter, a symbol, perhaps, of his growing ambivalence to the role he played in the devastation of the war. Silent throughout the rest of the conflict; silent during the aftermath of the war in Germany; silent in his emigration to Canada. All through those years he lived in Bridgeview, among his memorabilia and his commendations, he wondered: What had become of that pilot? Did he ever make it back? Was he spared, and the lives of the other men on his plane?

It wasn't until the '90s, when he read an article in a German pilot's newsletter, that Stigler's hopes for the survival of his "comrade" in the air were confirmed. The other pilot's name was Charlie Brown, it turned out, and for years he had been looking for the German humanitarian who had spared his life and the lives of his injured crewmen. Brown is interviewed in the TV report as well, and describes his joy when, in answer to his query, he receives a letter "all the way from Canada ... Surrey, British Columbia!" His eyebrows wag, as though to express how unlikely a place he considers this to be. The two finally met and became fast friends until their deaths, only six months apart, in 2008.

In the scene back in his Bridgeview home, Stigler picks out a cross dangling from a green taffeta ribbon. This one he's only recently received from England, a post-war peace medal, awarded him "because I didn't shoot Charlie down," he says with some pride. "It's the only one I'm allowed to wear."

Land Claims, Whose Claim?

> *I believe that the education of what happened to First Nations people should be taught in schools, starting at the elementary level.... My kids were taught nothing about it.... I have spoken at different events and talked about residential schools, and people come up to me and say, "I didn't know about that." It's just a shame.*
> — RHONDA LARRABEE

Down in Bridgeview, and on the North Shore, an ambiguity about whether you could stay or go, whether you were to be thrown out or were permitted to remain, though the conditions of your settlement might be dire, was playing itself out on a grand scale in the 1970s. And it was ghosted by a story of disinheritance that seemed to belong to a distant past, even as it structured the very terms of the present conflicts.

Much of the Fraser Valley was populated by people of the Kwantlen First Nation in the pre-colonial era, and where New Westminster and Bridgeview now stand, straddling the Fraser, were the Qayqayt — an Indian band that had built houses, fished, and hunted in the area up until the 1820s, when Fort Langley was established on a knoll of high ground to the east by European settlers. Taking advantage of the heightened opportunity for trade, the Qayqayt moved upriver to live nearer the fort. In 1879, as the cadastral maps of the Fraser Valley were about to be surveyed in preparation for large-scale settlement by Europeans, the federal government established three reserves for the Qayqayt (then known as the New Westminster Indian Band): one each on the north and south banks of the Fraser (including a site near Bridgeview), and a third on Poplar

Island, used by the First Nations as a burial ground. In 1900, smallpox (brought by Europeans) killed most of the four hundred members of the Qayqayt, and in 1916 the reserves in and around the Bridgeview and Westminster area were discontinued, "cut off" by the federal government, scattering the remaining Qayqayt to be assimilated into other reserves. By the 1970s, no trace seemed to be left of the original residents of the banks of the Fraser, nor any memory of the parcels of land accorded to the Qayqayt in particular, those reservations that had survived for less than forty years before they were erased to make way for exclusively European development — the British-styled city of New Westminster, with its royal airs, bustling commerce, and federal penitentiary, and across the river the residential neighbourhoods of Brownsville and South Westminster.

A civilization of previous inhabitants of the territory Europeans dubbed "Surrey" survived in name only as far as I was concerned, so ignorant was I of the history of the area we had just moved to. On the rare dry days of spring, as the weather warmed up, we were let out of our school into Kwantlen Park for our group exercises, in view of a stand of evergreens on a low hill, a fenced-in swimming pool, and some municipal tennis and lacrosse courts. As was the case across North America, tribal names had grown familiar on the tongues of European settlers over the decades as the identifying monikers of their schools, recreational complexes, Girl Guide packs, and Masonic chapters — even as the originators of those names were thought to have receded into a distant past. My first hockey-player boyfriend, for instance, belonged to an organization called DeMolay, a kind of Masonic outfit for "the fellow between the age of 14 and 21 who has dedicated himself to God, his country and his parents." It seemed that he and his older brother were always preparing for the latest "installation" of their officers, from the senior councilor through the standard bearer and the sentinel right down to the Chapter Sweetheart, a sacred position held at that time by a demure freckled brunette, who could be seen posing, head modestly ducked, beside the newly installed officers in the next day's paper. Prizes had been given out as well, including a "ritual proficiency trophy" to reward the boys' willingness to carry on the civic traditions of their fathers under the banner of the Royal Kwantlen Chapter of the Order of DeMolay. It is perhaps the affixing of the "Royal," which I rightly associated with British rule, to the "Kwantlen" that smudged my consciousness of the Native origins of that name.

Any modern-day story of suburban land-use battles, shorefront property disputes, squatters' claims, and eviction threats, any drama of whether one stays or goes from a piece of land one has occupied, is structured by this not-so-distant backstory of Native tenancy and displacement on the land.

In the case of the squatters on the Maplewood Mudflats, for instance, one of the reservations established in the nineteenth century has existed up to the present day. This is the Burrard Reserve, where the Tsleil-Waututh were accorded their bit of territory after previously enjoying full use of the foreshore for centuries prior to European settlement. At some point during their battle with the mayor of North Vancouver District, the mudflat squatters found allies among the Burrard people next door. One of the films features an interview with Len George, son of prominent Native activist and movie star Chief Dan George. In support of the squatters' own bid to prevent further development of the area, twenty-three-year-old Len George alludes to a plan to put in a Native land claim for the mudflats, since no formal agreement had ever been reached to transfer the North Shore of Burrard Inlet from First Nations to colonial ownership.

The film is vague. You have to turn to the *Vancouver Sun* for background, where George explains that the claim would be based on aboriginal rights because all the shore front land between Second Narrows Bridge and Indian Arm once belonged to his people. "There has never been a settlement or treaty for the land," he said. "There was a verbal agreement through my great-grandfather before 1890 but the whites just trickled in and he never bothered to tell them to go away because there was plenty of room for everybody."

If the Crown simply seized the land, making no agreement with the people who had populated it, and then the whites just "trickled in," was it not tantamount to a form of squatting? Who was to say that North Vancouver had the "right" to evict the latest wave of residents on the North Shore beach if the District's own claim to the land was itself on spongy ground?

"I'd like to see the Indians get it back," Len George says, "because it would stop industry and building down there and everything. It would set it back for I don't know how many years." Why would it set it back? "Because our financial place isn't that high, you know. It's going to take a while before this is all developed. And it would preserve the land a lot longer."

The *Sun* reported that George planned to "approach the B.C. Union of Indian Chiefs today to formally launch a claim." Whether the chiefs refused or the claim was unsuccessful is not clear, but nothing seemed to come of it. However, the fantasy scenario on offer here is novel: it was not the "Indians" who would be benevolently "taken care of" by a white bureaucracy, but, rather, a subcultural white community that would evade dispossession if the Tsleil-Waututh could re-annex what was, all along, rightfully theirs. Once having enlarged their reserve to include the mudflats, their meagre financial standing, as George put it, would act as a retardant on industrial and commercial development.

Down on the Fraser River it was a different story. Because the New Westminster Indian reserves had been discontinued, their inhabitants dispersed elsewhere, there was no nearby population of prior claimants to the Bridgeview land to trouble Surrey's official administrative authority over the south shore of the Fraser River.

Only retrospectively, from the twenty-first century, has a Native claimant to the land re-emerged from the obscuring grid of the European surveyors' map. Rhonda Larrabee thought she was of Chinese descent all her life, having grown up in Vancouver's Chinatown with what seemed to be Chinese parents. But it turned out her mother was a descendant of a family of Qayqayt who had lived on the New Westminster reserve before it was closed down.

> 'I'd like to see the Indians get it back.'
> Len George.
> **Mudflats Living**

An orphan, her mother was sent over two hundred miles east to Kamloops to attend a residential school, where she was forced to abandon her native language. When she came of age, she moved back to Chinatown with her sister and married into a Chinese family, effectively obscuring her Native history. Having uncovered this story from her mother's past, Rhonda researched her own Native roots, travelling to Ottawa to learn the history of her band. As of 1994, she became the first known living member of the Qayqayt, reviving the existence of a people thought to be long vanished — and subsequently raising the question of whether she would put in a claim for a land base on behalf of her people.

In the early '70s, then, when it was thought that no Native peoples could claim the territory over which Bridgeview residents and the Town of Surrey were fighting, the prehistory of colonial land use was thought to be just that — a prehistory, over and done with. But Rhonda Larrabee's emergence these decades later made it evident that no current European settlement could claim an unambiguous legitimacy.

Relocation Schemes

Thus it was that each individual household in Bridgeview was faced with the question: to stay or to go? To stay meant to engage in what seemed like a never-ending battle just to get what anyone else in the municipality had, and, moreover, to put up with the stigma of living in filth in the meantime. To go, for many, would have meant giving up a house they had built themselves, and into which they had sunk their life savings.

The municipality seemed endlessly inventive in its talent for fashioning ways to make Bridgeview definitively inappropriate for residential living. Otto reminded me of those ditches again, and I pointed out that everybody in Surrey had ditches. They were ubiquitous. Yes, Otto said, except that our ditches were big —

> *because water goes downhill, the water from Whalley and everywhere else came down there, right? So at the end of what used to be called Liverpool Road, if you're at the Turf, from there on, straight to the river, there used to be a gate that allows all the collected ditch water from the community to go out into the Fraser, it channelled into the Fraser river from there.*

He reminded me that this gate is mentioned in the film, along with what happened to it during one of the rainy seasons: "They brought gravel trucks in and dumped gravel so the gate wouldn't work, and the sewage effluent had no way of leaving."

I go back to this scene in the film. It's a September Surrey council meeting, a confusing crosstalk of voices. One says, "... with raw sewage going into the ditches and presumably that is being dissipated into the river through clean, well-kept ditches ..." And another interrupts, "Well, if the ditches were clean and well-kept you might have a ..." and the first voice again, "Well I'm trying to be reasonable," and another voice, "... in excellent condition, yes, yes, after City Hall got down there and filled them in with ..." And now the camera focuses on Otto Sr., who confirms with no small tone of irony that "yes, the ditches are in excellent condition, they don't work period, you know," as a raucous laugh breaks out.

"Either way," Otto says. "The water can't get in and it can't get out."

Yes, they had flooding in people's yards, Otto Jr. said, because so much water from the hillside came down during the heavier rains. "But when you go and close off the control gates, well, it got really bad."

As studies continued to be carried out (the testing of the soil, the counting of the souls inhabiting the land, the measuring of the ferocity of their attachment to it), relocation schemes would bob to the surface and then float away again in the face of the residents' scorn. In one "three-phase" plan it was imagined that they would move, en masse, to Green Timbers, about ten kilometres southeast of Bridgeview. Green Timbers was British Columbia's first "timber reserve," where, after the last stand of Fraser Valley old growth was stripped in the 1930s, it was decided that one square mile should be reforested and remain in its "natural" state as a reminder of what forests used to look like — and as a place where tree species could be preserved. British Columbia's first attempt at reforestation, Green Timbers came under constant threat of disappearance as various development schemes, like condominiums and a sports stadium, lured mayors to consider deforesting the area again. It seems the proposal of a "Bridgeview-in-the-Trees" (which would afford no views of a bridge) was another of these thwarted schemes to diminish the forest.

Further digging in the Surrey council minutes reveals that a Surrey neighbourhood already in or near Green Timbers was having some serious hygiene problems of its own. In February 1971 the Green Timbers Community Association submitted a "lengthy petition" from property owners requesting sewers. Scarcity of topsoil in the district (which included 390 elementary students) prevented "proper disposal" so that "faulty septic tanks are operating in the area. People are illegally hooking their septic tanks to storm sewers," resulting in instances of hepatitis and the creation of breeding grounds for rats in the ditches. Did Green Timbers suggest itself to Surrey council as a potential resettlement area precisely because of its septic tank and ditch problems — as though a population tainted by its hygiene dilemma could only be relocated to another area already adulterated with human waste?

Refusing to leave their neighbourhood by the river, Bridgeview citizens came up with a counter-scheme that would permit them to remain in their houses and, at the same time, bid farewell to the municipality that was trying to displace them. Otto Sr. crossed the Pattullo Bridge to pay a visit to Muni Evers, mayor of New Westminster. If Bridgeview had once belonged to the Royal City across the Fraser as part of South Westminster, mightn't it regain that status? Perhaps Bridgeview should secede from Surrey altogether and join up with a more sympathetic municipality. According to Otto, Mayor Evers was "very friendly" to the idea.

"The time has come to decide whether we are residents of Surrey or not," Otto told Surrey council. "If not we'll get the hell out of here."

Up on the Maplewood Mudflats, another relocation scheme was entertained that seemed to appeal to both squatters and officials alike. News coverage of the battle between the residents and the North Vancouver District authorities alluded to it vaguely at first — negotiations were afoot with the federal government, Paul Spong said, to "take over a recently vacated BC mining town." If the mudflats residents moved there, they could base their economy on "village crafts," he added.

The mining town, it turned out, was Bralorne, about a hundred miles as the crow flies north of Vancouver, deep in the mountains. The discovery of rich gold veins in the mid-nineteenth century began the settlement of the Bridge River valley, in the Chilcotin range; claims and counterclaims crisscrossed the geopolitical development of the area, as dynamite and pickaxes tunnelled into the mountains. During the Depression, Bralorne flourished because of the stability of the gold market, which brought thousands of resource workers to the area to earn high wages in the almost one hundred miles of underground networks, where ore was still waiting to be carted away. By the late '60s the area was about mined out and, like so many single-resource towns, Bralorne was in decline.

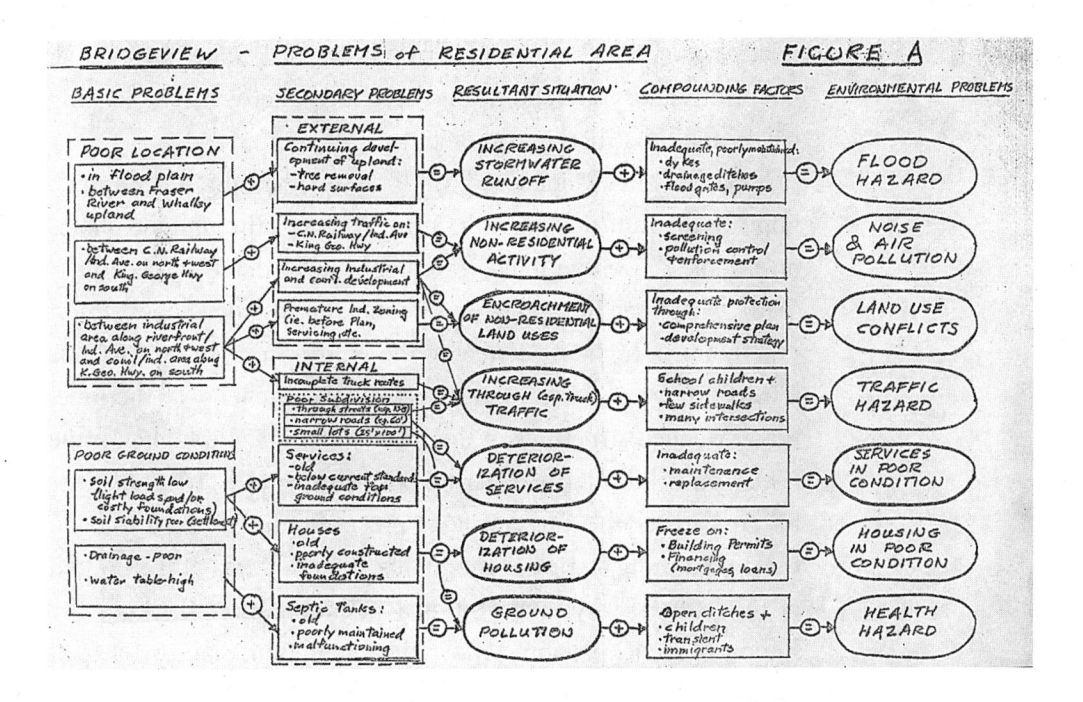

'Studies continued to be carried out.' Bridgeview — Problems of Residential Area. Flowchart from 'The Bridgeview Community Plan, Planning Department of the Corporation of the District of Surrey, 1976, Surrey Archives.

By 1971 it officially "closed" as a functioning mining town, but there were still hopes that someone else could make a going concern of it.

Advertisements touted Bralorne as the perfect ski getaway, for instance, featuring its iconic A-frame chalet — a larger, more appropriately set version of my family's A-frame on the King George. But not many vacationers could be convinced to make what was then an arduous (and at times impossible) drive so far north into the mountains, certainly not during snow season, especially when there was so much more convenient skiing close to home on Seymour, Grouse, and Whistler. Another ad simply seemed to be selling the entire town, offering houses, renovated or not, ready for immediate occupancy, and the opportunity to "run your own business if you like ... Stores, theatre, apartment block, gas station." The infrastructure was there already, "public highway, sewer, hydro, telephone, water, TV." It was first-come, first-served, but if you came you should "drive carefully" and "watch for logging trucks and construction equipment."

Apparently the Maplewood Mudflats squatters also offered some hope for the resurrection of Bralorne. As I click through the photos on Bralorne's website today (every ghost town haunts a website it seems), I can see the appeal — one shot, for instance, looks almost exactly like a high-angle view of the North Shore set of *McCabe & Mrs. Miller*: a shallow valley dotted helter-skelter with the functional wooden structures of the mining town, some higher, some lower, on a hillside interspersed with trees and debris, rail lines for ore carts connecting low-lying processing buildings, a wooden bridge spanning a crick or maybe just a muddy area at the bottom of the valley. Everything's muffled in snow. It weighs down the spindly branches of a lone pine in the foreground, makes white parallelograms of the roofs.

Dan Clemens said that the squatters formed the Gold Dust Twins Settlement Society, a "co-operative group which had been encouraged by the federal government to negotiate for the old Bridge River mining town of Bralorne as a model crafts community." The federal government? It was the Trudeau era (Pierre, not Justin), Clemens reminded me — "you know, the OFY era." By this he meant Opportunities for Youth, a federally funded program under the Liberal regime whose mandate was to find useful ways for the nation's young people to spend their summer months. Or even not so useful ways, according to one editorialist in our local paper, who lambasted the prime minister for suggesting that kiosks be set up across the country along the nation's highways and byways so that hitchhikers could thumb it from more sheltered, and safer, stopping-off points. We all love to travel, opined this writer, but not on the public dime. He thought the money would be better spent cleaning up "the ravines that run through Surrey," including the trash-choked creek behind our motel.

Drift, transience, relocation — it was on everyone's mind, some of it government-sponsored, some of it spontaneous. The Maplewood Mudflats squatters would move to Bralorne, along with some other arts communities in Vancouver, perhaps as part of a federal scheme to revive a ghost town. The idea seemed irresistible. This must have been what was on Willie Wilson's mind when, after musing on the rambling house he'd made with his salvaged materials, he remarked rather obliquely to the filmmakers that he was only going to take some "essential things with me, up there, 'cause I know I'll always be collecting something somewhere."

"Up there" is never explained in the film, but of course it was Bralorne he was imagining, up there in the mountains, where he'd build another rambling thing. The squatters would even take their shacks with them, or reproduce them once they arrived.

Clemens said, "I'd fantasize, through my experience in *McCabe & Mrs. Miller*, and the mudflats, and the Pleasure Faires — give me an island and put out thirty-million dollars for a movie set and let us live on the movie set when we're finished." He laughed.

Up in Bralorne, the idea was that the structures were part of a British Columbia architectural heritage — mining, logging, mountains, tunnels, flumes, booms. It was all part of the same picture for the Gold Dust Settlement Society. Though the gold might be gone, even the dust was part of history, a part of BC worth preserving. From the mudflats to the dust hills, they would revive the economy of Bralorne by returning to the small cottage industry of leather, beads, and precious-metal crafts. Everything seemed transferable. "I remember Paul [Spong] telling me he thought the killer whale could live in those lakes up there," Clemens recalled. The fantasy was that radiant.

It couldn't be sustained, of course, and a few days before the last squatters were burnt out, Clemens was quoted as saying, wistfully, that where Bralorne was concerned, "the government messed that up for us too." If an offer had been made, it was unmade just as fast, but not before the idea of a portable utopia had taken hold of the West Coast imaginary.

Stewards of the Environment

Squatting can begin as an opportunistic takeover of an idyllic liminal spot of land where you throw up your shack for a "time being," a time that feels boundless because unmeasured by monthly rent or yearly taxes, a time without calculation that seems to fly in the very face of mortality. But as the authorities draw near, a rationale is required; you have to put a spin on your otherwise unaccountable presence. It is for this reason, perhaps, that the more sympathetic news coverage began to portray the Maplewood squatters as stewards of a threatened environment, arguing that to wipe them out would herald the beginning of a wholesale destruction of precious wetlands.

In one news story ("Burrard Haven Threatened by Concrete: Squatters Fear for Mud Flat Wildlife") the squatters were portrayed "as part of a unique and harmonious eco-system that relies on their presence for its continued existence. They know if district council persists in its plan to push them out ... all the other creatures on the flats are sure to go as well." Willie Wilson described the estuarial nature of the place to reporters:

> We have a creek that runs through the middle of the mud flats — McCartney Creek — and it creates feeding areas by exposing the shrimp and clam beds. Every time the tide comes in it brings more food ... tiny crabs which feed on effluent. They are trapped in pools when the tides go out, and are eaten by gulls and herons.

A classic mudflat wetland, in other words, whose ecological value was incontestable. The squatters may have no legal "claim" to the land, Willie admitted, but "We belong here in the same way that the wild creatures do."

This sentiment is echoed by one of the reflective voiceovers in *Livin' on the Mud*, in response to a question we don't hear about the "wildlife" in the area. The voice is mildly defensive. "I don't know what you call wildlife," the speaker says. "Life, just life," as we see children paddling, herons, driftwood.

There is still actually wildlife here, within huge refineries across the way, those speedboats running out there, all those piles of logs floating around, the Dollarton highway the other side, that's living right in with the wild life. I don't know how wild you'd call it, it's pretty well trapped, it's doomed. We're, I guess, the tamest part of the wildlife. We will be about the first part to be wiped out.

This is what I mean about the melancholy of that whole scene, of those films, of the news articles — everything was always on the verge of being "wiped out," even as it was the best place to raise your kids, to nurture those bodies and those heads. There was something about the contrast, the proximity of the natural to the artificial and the "plasticity," as Paul Spong had put it, something compelling, something contradictory but endlessly fascinating, a paradox whereby the "natural rhythms" could only be placed in relief by the glow of the flare across the water, where the refinery steadily burnt off its waste, night and day, what Lowry had called "the red votive candle of the burning oil wastes flickering ceaselessly all night before the gleaming open cathedral of the oil refinery." For Spong, the mudflats were "the freest space I can imagine existing within the city ... surrounded on all sides by the city. You're totally aware that Standard Oil is right over there." The proximity of Standard Oil, Hooker Chemicals next door, Dollarton Highway, the log booms, barges, and freighters passing up and down the inlet — all this put their natural community somehow "within" the city itself, the debris of development and decay part of what made the mudflats both fecund and endangered. Some effluent feeds the tiny crabs, which in turn feed the birds, which in turn attract the martens and the raccoons; at the same time, the chemical plant's outfall wipes out all life for two acres around. "I found 30 dead ducks," Willie says. "They had been killed by an oil spill down at Port Moody." Or as Helen Simpson put it to a reporter, "You've got Hooker Chemical and Imperial Oil polluting here and the effluent coming around the corner, and they claim to be concerned about 27 people — who are probably healthier than anybody else — pooping into the water."

This human settlement was small, and the bodies of these twenty-seven people seemed fragile, not threatening, barely sheltered by their makeshift shacks. Leaving only the lightest of carbon footprints, their presence was now politicized as an environmental occupation.

Like the mudflats squatters, the Bridgeview residents, who had originally chosen that part of Surrey for its proximity to the river, combining the rural advantages of the river's edge with low-cost home-ownership, were now required to justify their presence in a place where they were not wanted. Perhaps it was his own idea, or perhaps it was the NFB animators who helped Otto Wittenberg firm up another plan of action: to make the argument that the low-impact presence of the residents in Bridgeview could function as a means to preserve the ecological viability of the area, more so, certainly, than the industry that was colonizing almost every available inch of the foreshore. This was a rationale even Lowry had spun out in his squatting days on the North Shore, where those "scattered folk who lived in [the cottages] year round were as good as unpaid forest wardens of what was not only a valuable stand of government-owned timber, but, unspoiled as the whole place was, with its paths and old cow trails, and older corduroy roads, here anyone was free to walk beneath the huge cedars and broad-leaf maples and pines, a sort of public park already."

Otto was interviewed near a sawmill, his sparse hair shifting in the breeze. "This used to be a nice area," he begins, as the camera backs away from a close-up of dark waves lapping at a dump site of charcoal-coloured shale to reveal a mishmash of logs strewn about, a long wooden building set up on stilts, flanked by a funnelled contraption with a slender smokestack — for burning scrap perhaps? All is set amidst a wasteland of recently levelled unpaved roadways, up against mounds of gravel and sand. Back before all this latest influx of industry, the river's edge was "not Stanley Park but, okay, it was sand. Kids could play here and all the rest of it," Otto continues as a front-end loader crawls past behind him, chuffing black smoke from its exhaust pipe. "But now you've got trucks, sand piles, machinery, and you've turned something that was in its own way beautiful into something that's really ugly." The wrong people are taking charge of the riverfront, he suggests, people who do not know the meaning of ecological stewardship.

"We have come to the conclusion that we would like to preserve this area for the people of Surrey to use for fishing or other recreational uses," Otto concludes, "because it's actually the only piece of Fraser River foreshore where access for the people could be made to the river." "A sort of public park," in other words, just as Lowry had envisioned.

South shore, foreshore, for sure. The refrain that Helen Simpson had incanted up on the Maplewood Mudflats was now being put into practice down on the south banks of the Fraser, on our industrialized mudflats. It took these working-class locals to stand up for what little river waterfront might be left in Surrey, where a viable fishing spot, or a place on the sand to spread out your picnic blanket, was getting harder and harder to find.

Scrap

Their light carbon footprint was not the only thing that qualified the mudflat squatters' presence on the North Shore as ecologically beneficial. Another was the salvage and recycle ethic they seemed to stand for with their rescue of architectural elements from demolition sites in the city, as embodied most obviously in the person of Willie Wilson. This collector of castoffs was integral to the films' message of making do with available materials, of repurposing the waste of modernization, a sort of ongoing reclamation project that flew in the face of the unbridled consumption that capitalism seemed to promote. This is what makes Willie one of the films' heroes, a gleaner of the world's excess.

It turned out that Bridgeview, too, harboured at least one such gleaner, and while *Some People Have To Suffer* makes nothing of his presence there as a collector of junk, it does offer a brief glimpse of him attending a meeting with representatives from the provincial government. He's the rumpled man, seen in profile, wearing an old wool pullover with a hole in the sleeve, asking questions of the politicians from Victoria in one of the film's grainy black-and-white process video sequences. It seems to take place in an institutional kitchen of some sort — maybe this is in the Bridgeview Community Centre? Otto confirmed to me that this man was Matt Wepruk, one of the unidentified residents in the film.

I knew about Wepruk even before I talked with Otto Jr. and had been hoping I'd find him in the movie. Each time the Bridgeview Committee turned up in the Surrey council minutes, it was represented by three core leaders: Otto Wittenberg, Alice Wilcox, and someone named Metro Wepruk, known by his friends, according to Otto, as Matt.

As I read through the many council minutes that mention Wepruk, I saw that his name appeared not only when he spoke on behalf of the Bridgeview Committee delegation, but also when the city was taking him to task for the junk that cluttered his premises. To whit: during a February 14, 1972, meeting, a letter was read out from the "Solicitor and Chief Inspector" regarding property owned by Wepruk: "The owner is continually piling old wrecks and cars" on this property, and "numerous charges have been levied in an attempt to correct this situation." As far as I can tell, the "situation" was never "corrected." Rather, Wepruk fought back with charges of his own. In October 1974 he appeared with the Bridgeview Planning Committee and expressed particular concern over a land-use application that proposed "industrial use of warehousing combined with townhouses" in one area of the neighbourhood. Wepruk "stated the proposed use was not compatible to residential use" and argued that "the outside industrial storage will be unsightly and they don't want that kind of development in Bridgeview." The Bridgeview Planning Committee instead demanded a "buffer strip between the industrial and residential uses."

Back and forth went the tug-of-war: in July 1978, council was on Wepruk's case again, this time citing the "Highways Scenic Improvement Act," under which they wished to have the "wrecked vehicles removed" from Wepruk's property. In August, council redoubled its efforts, resolving that "the accumulation of rubbish, garbage, ashes, filth, discarded materials and bodies or parts of vehicles or machinery located within Five Hundred feet of the centre line of 112B Avenue" (i.e., located on Wepruk's premises) was "unsightly or offensive to any part of the public travelling on 112B Avenue." This rubbish, therefore, must be "removed from the hereinbefore described lands and premises by the owner within 30 days of service of notification."

Wepruk must have stood his ground, and may have applied for a business licence, since by June 1979 the "Chief Inspector stated that the only course of action open to the Municipality is to license Mr. Wepruk at that location and require him to comply with the regulations on the Business License By-law." Council was reluctant to issue the licence, however, and voted instead to "appeal this matter in the courts."

None of these threats, warnings, and citations levelled by council at Wepruk seemed to make any impression on him as far as I can tell. Otto confirmed that the scrapyard existed right up until the last time he saw Matt, just a few years ago. In fact, he couldn't think of a time when it didn't exist, and he gave me instructions on how to find it. Let's say you are coming across the Pattullo from New West. Then, "if you just pass 128th, and you go up Peterson Hill to Whalley, you see Felix Scrapyard, and there was another scrapyard behind. That would be Matt's." I remembered Felix Scrapyard from the old days, with its sign featuring the rubbery, big-eyed Felix the Cat cartoon figure. Everything seemed sort of scrapyardish to me as you looked in that direction, so I didn't know to distinguish between the Felix and Wepruk properties. Even today, when you look down on the area from a Google Earth view, almost the whole riverfront east of the Pattullo on-ramp, with the exception of an undulating rectangle of grey gravel pits, is red with the rust of scrap metal outfits.

This poses a potential paradox for me: on the one hand, Matt Wepruk was a major player on the Bridgeview Planning Commit-

'Asking questions of the politicians from Victoria.' Matt Wepruk. Some People Have To Suffer

tee and, as we see, made cogent arguments for keeping Bridgeview zoned residential. Indeed, in his characterization of the core Bridgeview Committee, Otto described his father as the "spokesman" of the group and Alice Wilcox as putting in the "sober thought" kind of voice. Of Matt he said, "I remember no matter what it was, [Matt would say,] 'Let's just get 'er done,' a big smile on his face. 'I'll do that,' you know. So the do-er [of the gang]." Indeed, Metro Wepruk was sometimes referred to in council minutes as the committee's treasurer. He was key.

On the other hand, couldn't you say that Wepruk was the purveyor of the sort of business that contributed to the "industrialization" of Bridgeview? Or at least the piling up of the metal debris of industry, its "rubbish, garbage, ashes, filth, discarded materials and bodies or parts of vehicles or machinery," that had so offended city council? How was that in line with Bridgeview's desire to remain a primarily residential district?

I turned to the traces left by the neighbouring scrapyard, Felix Salvage, to help me with this conundrum. I didn't know how long Wepruk had been collecting and selling scrap in Bridgeview, and in any case, he was not as assertive about advertising his operation as

Felix had been — I mean, just the fact that I remember the prominent Felix the Cat sign as you came off the Pattullo attests to this. Felix, I know, had been around since 1950; the owner's solicitor said so in one of the council meetings. Felix Salvage had been established, it turned out, long before the bylaws that affected such businesses came into being, so it did not have to comply with those bylaws. The owner would, however, make an effort to keep the offensive scrap hidden from passing traffic by raising the fence and planting a few trees. But it was hard to limit the amount of salvage piled in the yard — this salvage was, after all, its inventory. Moreover, and here is where I think an argument is made that applies to Wepruk's scrapyard as well, the owner of Felix claimed that "the business was performing a service in Surrey by taking care of this junk."

After all, you have to ask, if Felix Salvage, and Wepruk's Salvage as well, were forced to get rid of all the junk on their premises, what were they going to do with it? Take it to the dump? Where it might rust and decay, but would not be put to any further productive use, either through repair, recycling, or smelting? When Surrey was finished with its tons of ferrous and non-ferrous metals, the scrapyards could be counted on to keep it circulating in larger systems of production and consumption. Moreover, the longer the lifetime of a useable metal, the less need for extracting more of it from the bowels of the earth. The junkyard man was the point at which waste was transformed into a renewable resource. This was the "service" provided by Felix, and Wepruk, to the municipality of Surrey.

But what of the scrap that was not rerouted to the realm of productivity and growth? The car parts and rusty machinery, the gears and bolts and greasy bits and pieces of industry gone to seed? When is it just "too much" junk piled on junk, kept on the premises with little likelihood of ever finding its way back into the useful stream of things? When the "collector" seems just as interested in the collection itself as in finding potential purchasers? With this image we find ourselves back on the mudflats in our encounter with Willie Wilson, Willie the Collector, cherished as much for the ethic of suspension, where his mass of objects is concerned, as for the reinstatement of their usefulness. Why couldn't Matt Wepruk be the Willie Wilson of Bridgeview? Is it the setting itself that turns a junkman into an artist? Is it that the context of the down-at-heels working-class neighbourhood is not the right background to give assembled detritus that special allure?

It is time to confess the circuitous route I've taken in my changing perceptions of Matt Wepruk. He has quite an extensive presence on the internet — more than you might imagine for a junkyard dealer who has not tried all that hard to flog his wares to a buying public. The first time I saw his name among the Bridgeview Committee members, either in the local papers or in the council minutes, I Googled him, of course, to see what I might find. This was before I talked to Otto about him. I was astonished to discover two accounts of legal cases, just a couple of years apart: in one Wepruk was the injured party; in the other he played the bad guy. These incidents took place in the twenty-first century, so at first I set them aside with the feeling that they were not relevant for my immersion in the '70s world I was exploring. In retrospect, though, I see that they coloured my understanding of Wepruk.

The first story was posted on a site called Narkive, a newsgroup archive where users post stories of interest to them. I couldn't tell where the news story had originally been published, though it was likely in the *Vancouver Sun* or another local paper. I assume it was a Narkive user who gave it the title "One Legged Man Awarded $280,000 in Damages After Confronting Meth Heads On his Property" — not a very journalistic headline, but colourful in a cheesy tabloid kind of way. The story itself was a pretty straightforward report of how the judge arrived at her ruling on the case, and provided me with a few details about Wepruk — the fact that he had lost a leg in a car accident in the '60s (which would explain why Otto told me he had a "tremendous limp"), that he had worked as a commercial fisherman, loved hunting, and was especially vigorous for a man of his age.

In the fall of 2000, some two-and-a-half decades after the ditch and sewer drama of the '70s, Matt was vexed that there had been several break-ins at his scrapyard. Suspecting that the culprits were "meth addicts" who lived near the yard, he went over one morning at 4 a.m. and took pictures of a red Pontiac Firefly parked outside what he knew to be their "drug house." The owners of the car saw him taking pictures, then followed him back to his own house. "Fearing for his safety," the article reports, "Wepruk grabbed a wooden post from his van and smashed the windshield and back window of the Pontiac Firefly. The Firefly was put into gear and drove into Wepruk, pinning him to the van." He sustained injuries that continued to plague him for the next four years, hence the judge's ruling that he receive damages, including an amount for "past loss of capacity to earn income." I found a follow-up ruling, suggesting that the owners of the Firefly appealed right up to the Supreme Court of Canada. It appears they had hoped that if they could prove Wepruk hadn't paid his income taxes in twenty years, he might be legally "barred from claiming income-related damages for past and future income loss." But the judgment was upheld, and the plaintiffs had to fork over the cash.

By the time this ruling was made, however, it seems that Matt had stepped up his measures to protect his salvage business — measures that led to an incident so lurid I hesitate to relate it. The twists and turns of the aftermath as they played out in court were instructive enough to earn a place on Michigan State University's Animal Legal and Historical Center website. That's where I read the whole unfortunate story.

It was 2002, and Bhagaoti Prasad, an elderly Fijian immigrant who lived with his family in Surrey and spoke little English, was working his way through the streets and avenues of Bridgeview as he had done for the past eight years; it was his delivery route for *The Leader*, the same local paper that had been carrying weekly stories of Bridgeview's battles back in the '70s. As Prasad walked past Wepruk's scrapyard, a dog came rushing out, went for his throat, and eventually took him to the ground, attacking him savagely. Neighbours called the RCMP but felt helpless to intervene between the dog and Prasad, the attack was so vicious. When the police arrived they pulled out their handguns and were preparing to shoot. Then Matt showed up, having been called at his house by a neighbour. The police instructed Matt to chain up the dog, but found Matt to be "belligerent and less than cooperative," expressing "disbelief that the dog would attack anyone." He did eventually grab the dog by the neck and walk him to the back of the junkyard, where he chained him up to a "heavy piece of machinery." While Prasad was rushed to hospital by ambulance, Matt (as he testified later) went to his tool shed at the back of the scrapyard and lay down for a couple of hours. No one was sure what happened to the dog; it, and the rusty chain that had insufficiently secured it, seemed to have disappeared.

I won't elaborate on the web of details in the case; suffice to say that when Matt was brought to court about the incident, he denied the dog was his. He said that he used to have a different dog, but this dog had been poisoned months before. A few of his neighbours testified on his behalf to confirm that he had previously owned this other dog, who was not aggressive at all but mild mannered, "like a child's dog." Nor had these witnesses ever seen the dog that attacked Prasad on Wepruk's premises. One witness described a morning when he had been repairing a motor in Wepruk's workshop and Wepruk came in "seeming distraught and told [him] that there was a problem out on the street with a dog or something"; then Matt lay down on the cot for a nap. The date on which this happened, however, did not match the date of the dog's attack on the paper carrier.

The evidence against Matt was pretty substantial, despite the testimony of his friends and neighbours: photographs taken of him with the attack dog "nuzzling the defendant's leg while the defendant scratches his neck" — acting, in other words, like a dog and its owner; the RCMP's testimony about how aggressive the dog was, and the fact that Matt had initially referred to it as his own before taking it to the back of the junkyard; the testimony of other neighbours who in previous months found the dog, even though chained up, so threatening that they avoided the scrapyard on their way to and from their homes. One neighbour commented that she had the impression "that the defendant kept the dog on the property to keep squatters and drug users away," and "now that the dog is gone, those kinds of people come more frequently to the area."

In the end, Wepruk was found "liable for the attack under the doctrine of scienter" and also "in negligence": that is, he knew of the dog's propensity for violence and should have taken better care to prevent its getting loose — provide it with a less rusty chain, for instance. Or even if he did not know, given that the neighbours knew how violent the dog was, he should have known. Prasad, the victim in this sorry tale, suffered extensive injuries and took a long time to recover. He was entitled, thus, to the heartbreaking sum of $3,300 in wage loss — given that his yearly earnings prior to the attack "were between $1,550 and $1,700" — and an additional $4,000 for future wage loss. For his "physical disability as well as ongoing psychological trauma" he was awarded an additional $35,000.

Aside from brief mentions of him in council minutes through the 1970s, this was the first substantial portrait of Matt Wepruk I had read, and it did not impress me favourably, to say the least. Shortly after I read the case involving the dog, I came across the story of his encounter with the "meth addicts," and I tried to make sense of the larger picture I was piecing together of a neighbourhood in which the residents, who themselves had been treated like "squatters" in their own municipality throughout the '70s (and beyond), were now (in the person of Matt Wepruk) taking up arms against incursions by a new wave of squatters, a down-and-out population, beset by addiction, who sought refuge in a literal scrapyard within the metaphorical scrapyard of Vancouver's industrialized edge territories. I had that Jim Croce song playing in my head all week, "Bad, Bad Leroy Brown," who's "badder than old King Kong" and "meaner than a junkyard dog." For some time this was the only way I could picture Matt Wepruk: a limping menace of a monster, not the owner of the dog but himself a junkyard dog. I couldn't help it, though I knew it was an impediment to rounding out a three-dimensional portrait of the man for myself.

Fortunately, Otto helped me get a sense of why Wepruk's neighbours would take his side in those scuffles with the law in his old age. I hadn't told Otto about the legal cases I unearthed — nor did he seem aware of them. I just asked him to give me a sense of Matt as he knew him back in the day. He'd already told me about his huge smile, his tremendous limp, his eagerness to do anything that needed to be done as part of the Bridgeview Committee. He was always dirty, Otto said, but, of course, "it was his job, he works in a scrapyard, he's always got grease and dirt and muck, oh my God, you know?" Otto made him seem more "rascally" than menacing. On Monday nights, Matt "didn't bother dressing up for council meetings ... just go as you are ...

> *And he had this habit of going up to all the council members, especially Vander Zalm, if he could, you know, he'd go and put his arm around him or his hand on his back, "How you doing?" and next thing you know there'd be a nice grease mark on the guy's suit.*

I was getting the picture, and I could just see Vander Zalm's aggrieved face, holding back his chagrin at being besmirched by the junkyard grime. You have to understand the kind of image our mayor had at this time. A spread in the *Surrey–Delta Messenger* in May 1970 sort of sums it up: Vander Zalm and his wife, Lillian, pose proudly under one of the long row of arches that frame the grand new house they've designed and built on 3.8 acres in the Port Kells area. "Home Theme Spanish for Vander Zalms" the headline informs us, before the story details the "attractive domed entrance hall, living room, dining room, kitchen, study, recreation room, workshop and four bathrooms." It's got Spanish-tiled floors, antique hardwood, a sunken bath, black ironwork chandeliers with amber glass — no salvaged leftovers for the Vander Zalms. There's even a handsome coat of arms in the main entrance, featuring an eagle with wings spread and two steel spears pointing down toward Lillian Vander Zalm's bouffant coif as she sits, hands demurely folded, on one of her black ironwork chairs, imported from Mexico. The house seems an appropriate showplace for a man who worked his way up from selling "ribbons and flower pots," not to mention a fulfillment of divine will. For as Lillian is "quick to say, 'God has placed Bill in the mayorship for a purpose.'" She explains that "she and her husband prayed prior to his decision to run for mayor. Both were determined to accept the outcome as God's will, no matter what."

Vander Zalm is, if nothing else, a man with a distinct idea about utopia. I don't mean utopia as embodied in his "themed" house so much, but as in something he says near the end of *Some People Have to Suffer*. Looking very thoughtful, he says that some have suggested that "we might just leave the area [of Bridgeview] and let attrition take its toll, and then as the people disappeared and as the houses were torn down because of age or otherwise, then it could be redeveloped to other use." This is not his idea, he states. Then:

> *Frankly, I don't know, and I don't believe anyone really does know now what the answer for the area might be, and perhaps I'm looking for Utopia, I don't know, but what I'd like to see done is that perhaps the services, if they're provided, that they should be provided in such a manner that, in effect, redevelopment can take place, if not now, at some future date.*

In other words, they could supply the desired sewers, thus quieting for the moment the constant din of those rowdy residents; but in an ideal world, the Utopian world, the sewers would be designed to accommodate the industrial development that would best exploit Surrey's riverfront resources, once the residents could be gotten rid of over the long run. Or at least that seems to me the point of this reference to Utopia.

It's safe to say that Matt Wepruk's house was not what you would call "themed," though it seemed to suit his needs and desires as fittingly as Vander Zalm's mansion fit his. Otto was blunt about this house:

> *Oh my God, the dump that he lives in, oh my God. It's just, echh, you know? But it was just the way he liked to live. Even to get to the front door was ... he had to walk through all the built-up scrap, metal scraps and junk ... it was horrible, you know. But it wasn't for poverty's sake or nothing.*

Not for poverty's sake. Otto's parents remarked to him many times over the years that there were a lot of people down there who "were not really as poor as the image they gave. They liked their lives there." This seemed to be the case with Matt Wepruk, who owned several residences in Bridgeview and in Port Mann, farther upriver. This property ownership seemed evidence, according to Otto, that Matt was not a poor man. He just liked his life in Bridgeview.

"You mean it was a place where he could live the life he enjoyed?"

"Yeah."

"And be left alone?"

It was not quite that, though Otto struggled with the exact words: "I guess you move up the ladder, you rat-race a bit more, and you lose . . ."

He didn't finish the sentence, but I think I know what he was saying, what could be "lost" as you climbed that ladder and furnished yourself with the trappings of respectability. Matt Wepruk did not give a fig for respectability. He liked his collected junk, he liked living with it, he just liked the whole environment it made around him. And in fact, Otto said, he could imagine Matt appearing on the *American Pickers* TV show; that would have been his people, his audience. If you showed up at his house, "he'd say, just a minute, I think I've got a 1950s grill in my backyard," and off you'd go to take a look at it. And so maybe among at least some of his neighbours, and for Otto perhaps, Matt was the equivalent of Bridgeview's Willie Wilson after all.

Human Settlements

In 1972, the year I started volunteering down on the Bridgeview flats, and the year the Maplewood Mudflats documentaries were screened for their first audiences, a seed was planted by Canadian delegates halfway around the world at the United Nations Conference on the Human Environment in Stockholm. The Stockholm meetings should be followed up, the Canadians proposed, by another conference focused exclusively on the global problem of how to ensure that everyone in the world had a decent place to live. Planning began almost immediately for what was to be the first UN Conference on Human Settlements, to be held in Vancouver, British Columbia.

During those preparatory years before what came to be known as Habitat, Vancouver was itself caught up in civic debates about development, livability, and an alarming housing shortage in the face of a rapidly increasing population. What better place to host a conference on the subject of adequate shelter for all? Could Vancouver be a model city for the world to consider, with its active port, its majestic views of the nearby mountains, its industry mixed with residential neighbourhoods, its radiant beaches, its recent commitment to "citizen participation" in development schemes for the city's future? Vigorous citizen involvement had recently averted the construction of a massive freeway project and a waterfront scheme that would have wiped out Vancouver's Chinatown and most of an historical residential district. At the provincial level, the newly elected Barrett government had just implemented an Agricultural Land Reserve, designed to freeze the sale of farmland for commercial, industrial, or residential development — an early recognition of how crucial it was to protect and promote local food production. City planner Harry Lash was working on an immense planning document, "The Livable Region," whose goal was to "manage the growth of Greater Vancouver" by finding out from the public "what livability means; abandon the idea that planners must know the goals first and define the problem; ask people what they see as the issues, problems, and opportunities of the region."

Chris Pinney and his social animators in Surrey were well aware of the emphasis being placed on citizen involvement in Lash's plans for Vancouver and its outlying municipalities. If livability was to be emphasized as a goal in the big city, part of Pinney's job was to make sure the less desirable aspects of urban life did not get shunted off to the southerly suburbs, where local politicians, like those on Surrey council, were all too eager to cooperate with developers seeking to make a buck on the refineries, landfills, and industrial parks that Vancouver did not want in its immediate backyard. And Bridgeview was the case study for this complex problem of livability in an urban context.

Mayor Bill Vander Zalm had made it clear that he was no Harry Lash, as evidenced in an interview in the *Surrey–Delta Messenger*. When asked whether he thought the municipality communicated adequately with the taxpayers, he replied, "What the people really seek more than anything else is leadership."

> *I think they want a council that is able to make their decisions [...] for them rather than all of this "input" we hear so much about. But contrary to what is being said regionally, and contrary to what many local municipal politicians think, I don't believe that the majority of people have time, or in fact, want all of this involvement that we keep hearing about.*

The Challenge for Change animators' work was truly cut out for them.

As soon as the UN Conference on Human Settlements became public knowledge, Pinney saw it as a prime venue to capture a global audience for our very local sewage problems down on the Fraser River flats. By October 1974 he was referencing the upcoming conference in his letters and reports about the Challenge for Change program in Surrey. "Later this fall," he wrote, "the Surrey project will be submitted as a project for funding under the Federal Department of Urban Affairs urban demonstration program. I am also hopeful that the project will, in addition, be accepted as a major demonstration project for the Human Settlements Conference to take place in Vancouver in 1976."

The Federal Department of Urban Affairs was established in 1971 to allow for a more direct relationship between Ottawa and municipal governments — and also urban citizens' groups — across Canada. It was via this federal ministry that citizen opponents halted the freeway project in Vancouver. In 1974 the ministry set up a special committee to "advise on the identification and selection of Canadian demonstration projects" for exhibition at the UN conference. Hugh Hanson, director of the committee, announced, "[These projects will] serve to improve the communities in which they're located, and remind Canadians that we have the ability in this country to tackle and solve urban problems, and they can — and probably will — be visited by many of the delegates to the Conference/Exposition while they are in Canada."

Meanwhile, in Vancouver itself, a kind of People's Forum was being planned for Jericho Park. This was to be a more accessible, citizen-based conference that would run simultaneously with the UN conference. If Vancouver city officials were hesitant at first to host the official conference downtown, given the cost of heavy security for such a high-profile gathering of international delegates, the Parks Board was even more reluctant to give the green light for a gathering of potentially unruly hippies in Jericho Park, which had already hosted the launch of Greenpeace actions and rock concerts. But through the tireless lobbying of Vancouver producer, filmmaker, and visionary Al Clapp, the People's Forum received the go-ahead:

> *With only five months' notice, he was able to organize 11,000 volunteers and unemployed students and tradespeople on work grants to refurbish the [park's] five art deco [seaplane] hangars into a beautiful village that was the earliest and probably still best example of public recycling in Vancouver's history. The hangars were turned into two beautiful amphitheatres for plenary sessions and performances, a hall for NGO exhibits on housing and sustainable technologies, and a massive social centre featuring the longest standup bar in the world entirely handmade with yellow cedar found on the beaches.*

Among the conditions the government imposed on Clapp to get funding for the forum was that he had to "use unemployed people. That wasn't a big problem," Clapp said later, "because most of the people I know and have worked with are what you'd call 'unemployed.' They're artists and craftspeople, who aren't what we'd call conventionally employed anyway. So it was a nucleus of some of Vancouver's most incredible artists."

Clapp had visited the Maplewood Mudflats in the early '70s and, in fact, had covered the squatters' plight for Vancouver's local media outlets. He was friends with Ian Ridgway, Dan Clemens, and the Deluxe Brothers "family" of carpenters and builders. They had collaborated on the Pleasure Faires, and now Dan and Ian were among the "unemployed" artists and craftspeople Clapp hired to transform Jericho Park's seaplane hangars into a showcase for their West Coast salvage aesthetic. "Ian had hangar number seven," Dan Clemens recalled. "I had hangar ten. As I remember, it was pretty amazing what we built. I don't remember much about the conference itself. My job was to build it, and I did. Ian built the 'world's longest bar.' Seven hundred feet."

I couldn't fault Dan for exaggerating the length of the bar, which was described elsewhere as snaking through hangar seven, Habitat Forum's "social centre," for almost 208 feet. It was the solidity, the beauty, and the bountifulness of the bar that was memorable. One Habitat visitor recalls:

> *It was made out of salvaged yellow cedar logs which were milled on site on a portable sawmill. The finished planks were a hefty three inches thick ... Sanded down and finished with several coatings of glossy varnish, the bar shone, and was the colour of a good chardonnay. Hundreds of thousands of people bellied up to it during Habitat's run that summer. It came to epitomize Habitat's human and smiling nature.*

It was as though Ridgway and his crew had combined the artistic and intellectual ambience of the Cecil Hotel's bar with the driftwood aesthetics of the mudflats to create a global watering hole for the world at the Habitat Forum. In fact, you could say that the whole shape and texture of Habitat Forum was incubated in the mud of the squatter's settlement on Maplewood. "That's another thing about the mudflats, you know," Ian told me.

> *I'd learnt all this stuff about how to build the English way, and then came over here and learnt how to build in the Canadian way, and then here's a whole other way altogether, which is just a bunch of old guys who want nothing to do with society, they find a driftwood pile and they just start to build themselves shelters, you know, and then we come along with our psychedelic attitude and want to do more of the same, even though we love the style, but we just augment it with stained glass and crystals and this, that and the other, done in strange ways. It's very recognizable.*

If Ian had learned the formal principles of woodworking in England, and enhanced them through his apprenticeship in Canada, it wasn't until he fell in with "old guys" like Mike Bozzer, the beachcombing pensioner with his antique handsaw, and joined forces with passionate "junk" collectors like Willie Wilson, that a distinctive Vancouver coastal building style could emerge and be put on display at Habitat Forum for the world to pass through. "Under the banner of Habitat," left-leaning planner David Gurin wrote,

> *two series of meetings were held in Vancouver, British Columbia, in June. One was the official United Nations Conference on Human Settlements that considered proposals which if made specific, and if implemented with lots of money could affect the way people live in cities and villages around the world. However, with the Arab-Israeli conflict lacerating the UN the specifics and the dollars from the rich countries are not likely to be available soon. Thus, the more realistic approach of the unofficial Habitat Forum became all the more interesting.*

The Habitat conference was rife with tensions from the start, most of them related to the stark economic divide between developed and developing nations — a conflict that was endemic to the United Nations in general. The themes of development versus livability, unsavoury sanitary conditions, relocation schemes, endangered ecological sites, and contested human settlements that were playing out locally on Vancouver's tidal fringes found full-blown analogues on the global scene. Uppermost in the minds of nervous Vancouver city officials, and in the press coverage of the conference, was the escalating international discord around Israeli-occupied — or disputed — territories following the Six-Day War of 1967. Maybe it was inevitable that a conference devoted to the global problem of "human settlements" would be coloured by these very prominent "settlements" on the West Bank. If the leaders of the developed nations wished to keep discussion focused only on the remediation of problems like housing shortages, access to services, and the need for clean water, seeking to treat the situation from the point of view of paternal benevolence — extending a helping hand to the needy — others, like the Group of 77, had a different approach in mind.

The Group of 77 was a coalition of developing countries, formed in 1964 with a view to improving their role in global trade. When Habitat took place, the UN had just adopted a set of proposals put forward by the Group, called the New International Economic Order. Habitat delegates who represented the Group of 77 worked vigorously to foreground the principles of the New International Economic Order in the Vancouver Declaration, the official document that had been drafted by the UN and was then heavily revised during the course of the conference. From the point of view of a developing nation, you could say that it was not possible to separate the question of adequate housing for all from the determining factors of geopolitical forces: colonialism and neo-colonialism, capitalist exploitation, apartheid, and the like.

Who had the authority to make decisions about how vast populations were to be safely and humanely housed in the locality that most suited them? Should the development of the world's cities — where the question of habitation was most pressing — be left to the developers, planners, and multinational corporations? But what of the millions of people who had, in the direst circumstances, made do for themselves? As Habitat's Secretary-General Enrique Peñalosa pointed out, in his own country (Colombia), "90% of all housing was constructed, not by the government or by the private sector, but by the poor themselves — often against the law."

There were forum papers on appropriate economic growth, the future of metropolitan areas, housing in developed and "underdeveloped" countries, human settlements and education, land-use strategies, indigenous building methods in the Third World; workshops on children and human settlements, hardcore poverty, health, quality of life for the handicapped; discussions about the arts, recreation, energy, and "the role of tall buildings" in human settlements; a prospectus for a "Self-sustaining Neighborhood-centered Community Development Corporation for Collection and Recycling of Household, Apartment House and Business Waste";

and a paper on the "Impact of Space Colonization on World Dynamics." Presentations were given on national settlement policies in Africa, Mexico, and Southwest Asia; urban renewal in London, Italy, and Liverpool; and the Mackenzie Valley Pipeline Inquiry in Yellowknife (the latter by the president of the National Indian Brotherhood). There was a session on women's role in shaping the urban environment. Considerable attention was also paid to the existence of squatters' communities across the world, and the question of how best to support their efforts to help themselves.

Most controversial, it seemed, was the emphasis placed on public ownership of land — both in terms of how that land should be utilized within a given country, but also in terms of a state's control over land that might be owned or occupied by foreign interests. The final version of the Vancouver Declaration addressed public ownership of land head-on. Since "private land ownership" was a "principal instrument of accumulation and concentration of wealth," contributing to "social injustice," public control of land use was "indispensable to its protection as an asset and the achievement of the long-term objectives of human settlement policies and strategies." Governments must maintain "full jurisdiction and exercise complete sovereignty over such land with a view to freely planning development of human settlements throughout the whole of the natural territory"; moreover, land as a natural resource "must not be the subject of restrictions imposed by foreign nations which enjoy the benefits while preventing its rational use."

As if to drive home the point, the next section insisted that "in all occupied territories, changes in the demographic composition, or the transfer or uprooting of the native population, and the destruction of existing human settlements in these lands and/or the establishment of new settlements for intruders" was "inadmissible"; policies that violated the protection of heritage and national identity "must be condemned." Among the general principles of the declaration was the affirmation that "every state" had the "sovereign right to rule and exercise effective control over foreign investments, including the transnational corporations — within its national jurisdiction, which affect directly or indirectly the human settlements programmes." The establishment of settlements in "territories occupied by force" was illegal and condemned by the international community — "however, action still remains to be taken against the establishment of such settlements." Highest priority was to be placed on "the rehabilitation of expelled and homeless people" who had been "displaced by natural or man-made catastrophes, and especially by the act of foreign aggression."

The Vancouver Declaration included a list of resolutions to be voted on by delegates, which would form the basis for amelioration of the global crisis around human settlements going forward. But after much debate on a number of contentious issues, it seemed impossible to reach a consensus. For one thing, powerful developed nations like the United States took exception to the declaration's emphasis on a New International Economic Order. Even more crippling to broad approval of the declaration was a statement that had been included, taken out, and put back in several times over the course of the two-week conference: this statement echoed a resolution adopted by the UN a few months earlier, which asserted that Zionism was equivalent to racism. As might be expected, this claim was unacceptable to Israel, which therefore refused to agree to a document about human settlements that took an explicitly hostile stance towards its current policies. Israel's opposition to the declaration as a whole set a precedent that was followed by most of the other developed nations. The final vote was 89 in favour, 15 against, and 10 abstentions — a split, in other words, between the developing and socialist nations on one side, and developed countries on the other. The irony for Canada (which had lined up with its neighbour to the south) was that it could not vote in favour of the work that had been accomplished at the conference hosted by its jewel of a West Coast city.

If Vancouver's civic leaders felt less than sanguine about the media emphasis on the Middle East conflict that their conference was drawing, they were doubtless none too happy either with Habitat Forum's strong focus on — indeed, its living example of — the radical politics of "self-help housing." This is the kind of housing you might find in a squatter's community, for instance, and is also known as "construction by the informal sector." The refurbished seaplane hangars, retrofitted with salvaged materials and beautifully constructed in just a few short months through the cooperative efforts of unemployed youth and former squatters, contrasted sharply with the concrete, glass, and steel skyscrapers that were beginning to dominate the cityscape downtown. As David Gurin put it, Canada had "sponsored the Habitat Conference while planning the destruction of some of its own best habitats," Vancouver itself being "a sad example of this":

> *Its setting along an indented harbor beneath stunning high mountains is perfect. Its recent city planning is something else. Multinational and Canadian investment schemes pulverized the old downtown of the city. Diversity and street-level activity were wiped out to make way for high-rise offices, hotels, and apartment buildings, separated by meaningless empty plazas.*

Even though the city itself did not "offer the best example to the world," Gurin went on, "some of the people who made Habitat Forum into a two-week university of human settlements taught very well indeed." He praised it as a "monument to self-help," noting in particular the "wooden arcades designed in Canadian Indian motif" that led from each renovated hangar to the other — resonating, perhaps, with the wooden boardwalks that had connected the squatters' shacks on the mudflats a few years before.

The countercultural, imaginative, and festival-like physical setting of the forum at Jericho, and the informal conversations that were nurtured there, formed the matrix out of which "spontaneous urban settlements" could be explicitly emphasized in the official Vancouver Declaration. Residents of such "unauthorized" settlements, the Declaration stated, "frequently organize with the intention of providing their communities with essential minimal services." Since these services were often difficult to "obtain without assistance," governments were urged to "concentrate on the provision of services and on the physical and spatial organization of spontaneous settlements in ways that encourage community initiative and link 'marginal' groups to the national development process." This included the provision of "appropriate forms of public assistance to individual or co-operative self-help efforts."

By "self-help efforts," could the Declaration mean efforts like those engaged in by the Maplewood Mudflats squatters or, indeed, the residents down in Bridgeview, who were contravening the law by attempting to fix their leaky roofs while a public health ban was in effect?

The Performative Art of Squatting

By the time the Habitat conference and Habitat Forum took place in 1976, the squatters were gone from the Maplewood Mudflats. I have mentioned that both the mudflats films end with flames of destruction. While many of the shacks were summarily bulldozed by North Van District authorities, the last few were torched in sensational, televised bonfires just before Christmas 1971. Helen Simpson, completely exasperated by this time, took matters into her own hands and set the house she had lived in for four years on fire. "I'm glad we did it ourselves" she was quoted as saying. "I didn't want any of them [meaning National Harbour Board employees] to go near it."

Linda and Paul Spong's house also burned. Paul wasn't there at the time. He was "in Ottawa, putting poetry under Trudeau's door." Linda told me this as we watched the flames at the end of one of the films. "I don't know what his poetry was," she said. "Maybe a request, like [and here she switched to a tiny voice]: 'save the mudflats.'"

"And who burned your house?" I asked.

"The mudflats people decided, well, we're going to burn it, we're not going to let them have the . . ." She broke off, remembering. "I knew it was going to happen, and I even watched it burning. Then I went away for a few hours, and I came back, and I knew how a wasp feels when they take their nest. This is pretty shitty. It was like, wow, like a divorce. Even though you're ready for it, you're never ready for it."

For Tom Burrows it was a different story. He had rivalled Paul Spong for inventiveness in the squatters' showdown with North Vancouver District officials. Discovering at one point that there was a disparity between the two entities claiming to control the foreshore where his shack was located, Burrows staged a bit of theatre to draw attention to the absurdity at the root of so many land-use skirmishes.

> We noticed that the boundaries of the two parties who purported jurisdiction over the flats did not match-up. Their individual land surveys, that of the Corporate District of North Vancouver and that of the National Harbours Board, had been completed several years apart. They should have joined evenly on the mean high-tide line but alluvial fill from the creek running beside our shack had created an oblong shaped piece of land that neither party claimed. It was large enough to contain the shack, 90 feet out in front on the flats.

Tom got his artist friends to help him lower the shack onto driftwood rollers and move it to the unmapped area of the shore.

> Close to Xmas, court order in hand, the building inspector of the Corporate District of North Vancouver led a crew to the flats to demolish the skwat. Our shack was roped off in an area with signage declaring No-Man's-Land. Feeling humiliated by the protracted trial and horrified that it might begin again, he snapped. The inspector torched the shack, corporate arson.

But not before Tom's story had been covered in the *Vancouver Sun*, on the same page as that Bob Hunter column on "female chauvinist pigs." While it may not have saved his dwelling, the manoeuvre demonstrated the capriciousness of manmade boundaries and what they stand for. In this case, "Nature" itself had trickled in with its alluvial wild card, seeming to nullify cartographic law and offering a loophole through which Tom's shack could slide into safety. That the city official torched it anyway was evidence that under the surface of rationality was a crime of passion waiting to happen: "corporate arson." If he had "snapped," the result nullified the entire legalistic basis on which the squatters were being evicted in the first place.

By the time Habitat preparations were underway, Tom Burrows had made the art and politics of squatting an intrinsic element of his creative practice. Now a founding faculty member of the new BFA program at the University of British Columbia, Tom remembers he started "collecting archival material and lecturing on the history of squatting in Vancouver" throughout the early 1970s. "I was presenting the mudflats as a form of social sculpture," he recalled. "I had good archival material, images." It was a way of contextualizing his own experience on the mudflats, of linking his squatting activities to more global phenomena, even as he recognized the significant differences between the North Shore artists' colony and self-built settlements in the slums and favelas of the developing world.

If anyone could be called an expert in the performative art of squatting, it was Tom Burrows. So when Bruce Fairbairn and Charles Haynes (who soon after published a book titled *Self-Help Housing*) began preparing a symposium on self-help architecture for the Habitat Forum, they invited Tom to contribute an art installation that would complement it. Haynes and Fairbairn, Tom's colleagues at UBC, "were showing people how to get their thing, build their own communities, build their own architecture, and I had this thing on dealing with squatting, and somehow they were put together," Tom recalled. "So I built a kinda from my research, I built out of some rusty corrugated iron and stuff, built this kind of third-world squat, and I poured ammonia all over the floor so it smelled of piss [he laughed] and had documentation that I could find, and people coming in."

Was the odour of urine to ensure that Habitat Forum visitors got the full, Sensurround experience of what a self-built dwelling might be like in a third-world locale, where resources had not yet been extended to help a squatter attain ideal sanitary conditions?

Whatever the intention, Tom said he was "astounded by what showed up," meaning representatives from all over the world who were involved at various political squatting sites — in particular, members of the Situationist movement in London, a movement Tom knew from his student days there in the late '60s. Habitat Forum was the convergence point for all the international pioneers in the newly emerging movements around self-help housing, beginning with John Turner, whose 1972 book *Freedom to Build* (co-authored by Robert Fichter) was a kind of primer for the symposium on the importance of helping squatters help themselves. The blurb on the cover of Turner's book summed it up perfectly: "From their worldwide experience the authors show that where dwellers are in control, their homes are better and cheaper than those built through government programs or large corporations." Over a thousand conferees, from over forty countries, signed up to form a "Network for Local Housing Action," proposed by Turner as a global network that would help community activists in developing nations find desperately needed support from experienced peers. "The actual or threatened destruction of communities can sometimes be averted by local action when supported by professionals and politicians," Turner wrote, "and the latter can be supported, in turn, by more fortunate people like ourselves."

Also present at the Habitat Forum was Egyptian architect Hassan Fathy, famous for helping to build New Gourna, a settlement on the west bank of the Nile that combined traditional earthen materials with modern architectural principles. Fathy "explained how to use local materials, local technology, and local labour for 'no cost housing.' He showed slides of Egyptian peasant homes, graceful and durable with vaulted mudbrick roofs."

Inspired by the efforts of activists like Fathy, who were working with squatters on the other side of the planet, Tom Burrows saw the next phase of his artistic trajectory opening before him: with the support of grants from the United Nations and the Canada Council, he took off in 1977 on a seven-month pilgrimage to squatters' communities around the world and created a series of documents — photographs and typed placards — testifying to the ubiquity and seriousness of self-built human settlements as a global phenomenon.

He visited social anthropologist John Clifford, who had become a "petty criminal" to live among the pavement dwellers of Calcutta. He covered the forceful eviction of a group of Parisian squatters on the day before the trêve d'hiver, or winter truce — the informal law that no one could be forced from shelter during the frigid months between November and March. He collected photographs of the very politicized squatters' movement in London, where a hundred thousand units lay vacant during a severe housing shortage, and where thirty to fifty thousand squatters were met sometimes with evictions, sometimes with services from the local councils. England's newly passed Criminal Trespass Law, Tom wrote, was eroding three-hundred-year-old squatters' rights. In Bangkok he witnessed the efforts of a community activist to bring firefighting skills and equipment to slum-dwellers who were routinely cleared out by the same kind of state-sponsored arson that had engulfed his own squatted shack. He visited "Freetown Christiania," a former military base in Copenhagen that had been taken over by youth in 1970 and had grown into a collective settlement of about a thousand residents. "Denmark is a social welfare state based on the nuclear family," Burrows wrote. "There is a very high suicide rate. Something is rotten in Denmark. Youth seeks an alternative." He dropped in on Amsterdam, where squatters had "become a potent element in the theatre of city planning" by defending the "indigenous character of Amsterdam's varied neighbourhoods in opposition to the exploitation of property speculators." In Rome he took photos showing how "obscure political parties squat buildings as their headquarters: the women's movement squat buildings to have a base of action ... [and] construction workers move their families in and squat luxury apartments that they have just built with their own labour." He documented a cooperative of itinerant street artists in New Delhi, noting their successful demonstrations to repeal the anti-begging law.

When he caught up with Hassan Fathy's experiment in "New Gorma" (as he termed it), he found the settlement Fathy had helped build in the 1940s, and which had been vacant for thirty years. By

'Corporate arson.'
Tom Burrows's house on fire in the Maplewood Mudflats, torched by the North Vancouver District Building Inspector, December 1971.
Collection of the Morris and Helen Belkin Art Gallery Archives, University of British Columbia, Tom Burrows Fonds

the '70s it was being re-inhabited by the overflow population from nearby "Old Gorma." "These squatters," Burrows wrote,

> make a living from people like myself who come to see Fathy's work. The squatters' background is generations of grave robbing within the privacy of their homes [which had been built over ancient burial grounds]. They have a different idea of architectural details, such as small shuttered windows rather than Fathy's esthetic arches. The squatters have their own mud-brick yard for materials to alter Fathy's prescriptive architecture.

The irony was so obvious Burrows barely needed to emphasize it, merely noting that the squatters were "destroying the architecture from which they are making their living. Extensive social anthropology," he drily concluded, "is necessary when one is dealing with a clientele outside of one's class or culture."

Burrows's exhibit also included materials depicting Hans Haacke's exhibition prepared for, but cancelled by, the Guggenheim in 1971 — a documentation of "the slum property holdings of influential people attached to the Guggenheim."

And he presented his own experience on the Maplewood Mudflats in the context of the history of waterfront squatting in Vancouver dating back to 1900. "In Vancouver Canada, people built squatter homes on the tidal-land of the harbour where it was difficult to define the legal boundaries of property between the land and the ocean," Tom wrote. "These squatter homes worked as an alternative to privately owned property in times of individual or public economic stress. The fact that these homes were privately built utilized the resources of individual peoples rather than a welfare state." In 1940, he noted, "it was estimated that there were 20,000 squatters; one tenth of Vancouver's population." Since that time, "these foreshore squatter-communities have all been destroyed in the name of progress. I lived in the last of these communities before it was razed by civic authorities in 1971."

One of his photos showed Ida and himself imitating Grant Wood's iconic American Gothic, but with Tom holding a broom rather than a pitchfork, and the two of them standing waist deep in a perfectly round hole cut out of the floor in the kitchen of their home on the mudflats. "I chain-sawed the hole," Tom told me when I asked about it, "to insert a circular bath tub (with drain) filled from pans of water heated on the stove, and covered with a trap door when not in use." A grainy black-and-white snapshot showed the exterior of the cabin, its clapboard siding and window frames in silhouette against an overexposed white conflagration inside, roof engulfed by the flames exploding upward into the sky. Tom had affixed the words "my house," in unevenly lined-up Letraset, to the centre of the blaze. It was the "end of a way of life," his Vancouver placard announced, but also "The beginning of another?" Who could tell what the 1980s would bring, now that the housing crisis in Vancouver was worse than ever.

After his travels, Burrows prepared his informational placards and mounted the photographic images, like so much evidence, on simple pasteboard — no formal framing — to facilitate ease of transport and adaptability to any exhibition context. Quotations from John Turner and Geoffrey Payne, "one of the most articulate of the new generation of third-world planning theorists," rounded out the exhibit. Tom titled it "Skwat Doc" and stuffed it all into a modest briefcase, as though to emphasize its portability.

His aesthetic rationale framed the project in terms of how what he called "3-D systems" (architectural structures that we call housing) might be imposed by larger power systems, but were also malleable in the hands of those who occupied them. The dominant or mainstream versions of these 3-D systems were fixing people "to an existence that is static, without options."

> *I have chosen to explore squatting as a factor in the housing system because it is an option that is in reaction to the static existence. Squatters most often occupy an area when the options given by the amenities where they choose to squat are more important to them than their assured tenure.*

In other words, people will choose to remain in a place that appeals to them, even if they must live under constant threat of eviction. To squat, he concluded, "is to act within the theatre of politics. It frees the participants' 3-D creative decision-making-processes within their immediate environment; the home, the community. It allows the possibility of multiple and serial choice. Squat is both an object and a verb."

Bridgeview at Habitat

Chris Pinney's film *Some People Have To Suffer*, the documentation of Bridgeview residents seeking to exercise their "3-D creative decision-making-processes" down on the Fraser River flats, was ready just in time for the Habitat conference. It was shown as one of 230 film and slide presentations "brought by national and intergovernmental delegates, each attempting to discuss a specific settlement problem, a solution that was applied, and an evaluation of the solution." But Pinney was not content merely to screen his film and describe the Challenge for Change project as it was unfolding in British Columbia. If Tom Burrows had recreated a urine-scented simulacrum of Third World squats for the forum's self-help symposium, Pinney, too, was determined to bring home to delegates a much more visceral understanding of how economic interest led to standoffs between business friendly authorities and the residents under their jurisdiction. Or, rather, he was determined to bring the delegates home to the very habitat where the battle for sanitary conditions was being played out. So he hired a bus.

This is how I imagine the off-site excursion played out: UN delegates and other forum visitors finish up their beers at the Longest Bar in the World, then file outside where Pinney beckons them to clamber aboard a local school bus, cameras and notepads in hand. Pinney directs the driver to take them, not the quickest way, via the Trans-Canada freeway and over the Port Mann Bridge into Surrey's easterly township of Guildford, but through the commercial strips and residential neighbourhoods of Vancouver's nearest suburb, Burnaby, then on past the well-trimmed hedges of New Westminster, and finally over the busy two-lane Pattullo Bridge — the passengers craning their necks to catch a glimpse, as they speed past the bridge's orange girders, of the acres of log booms spread out on the Fraser below. In a moment they are on the other side, have turned off the King George Highway, passed Felix Salvage Company with its comic black cat gesturing toward mangled automobile carcasses, and arrived at an unprepossessing collection of down-atheel houses. The bus pulls into the elementary school parking lot, the same lot where the air had been let out of my bicycle tires a few years before. The delegates file out, taking care not to step in puddles from a recent late-spring shower. And then they go for a stroll out into the neighbourhood, alongside the ditches choked with the same weeds, trash, and debris they had just witnessed in Pinney's film. Maybe there is an odour, maybe not. Maybe Otto, Alice, and Matt show up to give a more personalized tour. For sure, Pinney has made his point: that the Third World they've been discussing so earnestly up in Vancouver is not on the other side of the globe. It's only twenty miles away, in Vancouver's own backyard.

The mayor and aldermen of Surrey were not amused. In fact, within a couple of weeks, at their June 21 council meeting, an indignant motion was made:

> *That any member of the T.V. media which does not intend to show an entire meeting, but instead does careful editing for release at a future date to support one or more particular cause or causes, does this Council and the democratic process an injustice and from this night onward, shall be excluded from filming the proceedings in this Chamber.*

The alderman who put forward the motion was not attempting to "censor the legal press or Channel 10," he said. He was concerned "over filming done particularly in relation to Bridgeview ... operating under federal Government Funds." This film, which unfairly "shifted blame for lack of sewers ... onto the Council rather than on the lack of support and funds from the Federal Government," was "shown at the Habitat conference in Vancouver." The National Film Board, fuelled by its "federal" bucks, and engaged in "careful editing," had proven itself to be an enemy of Surrey's authorities, yet another example of Ottawa sticking its nose in business that had nothing to do with it. After some discussion, the majority of the council members thought better of this desire to ban the NFB from council chambers, and the motion was struck down. But by now the Challenge for Change program had made its mark in Surrey and had established a Community Communications Centre at Douglas College, where local residents received training well into the 1980s in how to "carefully edit" the videos they shot, and take them to the local media, whenever their elected officials seemed not to have their best interests in mind.

Bridgeview Today

Some People Have to Suffer closes not with a bonfire but with a flood, the result of heavy rains in October 1975 during Pinney's last weeks of filming. As the camera pans across an elderly woman in her dress coat, gingerly making her way along an inundated street, or a car slowly plowing through the flood, sending up a sheet of water and dousing a nearby picket fence, or a child balancing on a piece of wood to keep from toppling into the drink, the film's voice over informs us that

> streets, schoolyards, and home basements were flooded with foul-smelling wastes containing coliform counts millions of units above safe levels. The municipality's own health board said Bridgeview had become a biological time bomb ripe for a major epidemic of pathogenic diseases such as typhoid and diphtheria.

But although the provincial government finally came through with a commitment of $2.5 million to help the municipality build sewers, Surrey council now decided that "Bridgeview needed a more expensive system, a system that could serve industry as well as the residential community." This was Vander Zalm's "utopian" solution, which amounted to yet another delay tactic. Even a change in local government did not seem to improve the situation. Ed McKitka, an alderman who had been portrayed as something of a working-class hero throughout the film, taking the residents' side against the businessmen and "housewives" who made up the rest of council, won the race for mayor, we are told, as Vander Zalm climbed his ladder up to the provincial legislature, where he became the province's Minister of Human Resources (and later premier). But even under McKitka's leadership, the council unanimously rejected "the proposal by their own Planning Department to include Bridgeview in a community rehabilitation program." And thus, for residents, "it was the start of another year of delegations, committees and negotiations." (I should add that British Columbians, and maybe even a lot of Canadians, will chuckle at the memory that after losing the mayoral election in 1977, McKitka was investigated for breach of trust while he was mayor and eventually convicted and given a three-year prison sentence.)

The film concludes with a freeze frame of a flooded yard, where a soccer ball floats over the inverted reflection of a Bridgeview bungalow. When a rolling text appears, as though tacked on at the last minute, announcing that the sewers are promised for the summer of 1977, we feel as skeptical as the residents must have been as they waited "to see if this plan would finally solve Bridgeview's problems."

After its premiere at Habitat, it is not clear how often, or in what circumstances, the film was screened for local audiences. Otto surprised me when he said that he hadn't seen *Some People Have To Suffer* until about 2006. When I asked why he hadn't seen it in the '70s, he said that they never knew it had been released. "My Dad told me," he recalled, "that he was told it was kind of just spirited out, it was never released."

The Wittenbergs might have missed the film because they finally left the neighbourhood in 1975, before its release — which meant they were not around for what I imagine must have been a gala screening for Bridgeview residents at the community centre. The story of their departure, Otto said, "was kind of funny." There had been an empty lot next to their home, "just blackberries and bramble," that was purchased by a Jehovah's Witness organization to put up a warehouse.

"They have these mobile trailer kitchen units for when they have conventions," he explained, "and so they built this large warehouse right next door to us, but they weren't allowed to use it (to store their supplies)."

Why not?

"Because they didn't have a toilet," he laughed, and I'm assuming they had no permit to build a toilet either, given what was happening at the time. "So they actually bought our place for the toilet." They offered Otto Sr. enough money that he was able to buy the family a new house in the more well-heeled municipality of North Delta, right about when Otto was graduating from high school.

But Otto's childhood in Bridgeview, and particularly his role as official documenter for the Bridgeview Committee during their battles with City Hall, had a lasting influence on who he became as an adult. "It's kind of interesting how things shape you," he said. For instance, he got "involved with the NDP" and was on the federal New Democratic Party's North Delta executive committee for over twenty years. He was also a mover and shaker in Canada's largest private-sector labour union, Unifor, where he had been president of the union local (433) since 2006. "And you think back, where does that actually come from, you know? And despite what you see in the film, my dad was very much an authoritarian character, so basically I've been fighting authority in many ways, finding different strategies for doing that." Fighting back against paternal authority, for sure, but also fighting with a sense of authority no doubt derived from that long, drawn-out war with Surrey council so many years ago.

One thing is certain: *Some People Have to Suffer* never achieved the star status of the NFB's *Mudflats Living* and its companion film, *Livin' on the Mud*, both of which functioned as what Bob Hunter would have called a "Mindbomb": popular media meant to revolutionize a generation's way of thinking about things. The Maplewood Mudflats squatters' community, preserved in these two melancholy films, was itself a kind of Mindbomb, infusing Vancouver's sense of itself as an urban environment distinct from its Canadian neighbours to the east, and its American neighbours to the south. But despite the obscurity of *Some People Have To Suffer*, the efforts of the Challenge for Change animators and, more importantly, the Bridgeview Committee members seem to have paid off in the end, or at least paid off for a few decades of more sanitary living conditions.

When I went to the new Bridgeview Community Centre in 2010,

I found an informational placard near the building's entrance; erected in 2003, it offered a brief tour of the neighbourhood's history, beginning with its settlement in the 1860s through the 1880s, when a ferry known as the *K de K* brought people and their wares across the Fraser to the city of New Westminster. There is a section on the "Bridges" of Bridgeview, and then a paragraph titled "A Community Taking Shape," in which the saga of the ditch and sewer battles is recapped, including the defeated Green Timbers relocation plan, the community's insistence on remaining, the growing "tension between the inhabitants ... and the Municipality," and the threat of secession to New Westminster. I wasn't sure what to make of the assertion that the sewers were installed in 1975, a date that appeared to be in conflict with the film. But in any case, according to the placard, the arrival of the sewers meant that "the tension subsided" — as though Otto Wittenberg's threat to join the Royal City was the deciding factor. In a final section, titled "A Sur-

'Bridgeview had become a biological timebomb.' Bridgeview during flood of October 1975. *Some People Have To Suffer*

viving Community," the construction of the new community hall seems to stand for Bridgeview's crowning victory over all odds. It is there, we are told, that events and programs for the "families of Bridgeview" are offered, such as an "annual Halloween Haunted House, a Christmas dinner, and an Easter brunch," a rather Christian list of holidays for a neighbourhood whose cultural makeup has become decidedly more diverse.

In the twenty-first century it looked like Bridgeview was qualifying once again for the ministrations of nationally based community-development projects — for instance, the Action for Neighbourhood Change (ANC) program. Sponsored by the United Way as well as some other philanthropic organizations, the ANC had in 2005 targeted Bridgeview as one of five neighbourhoods across Canada to benefit from a "learning initiative that explored and assessed approaches to locally-driven neighbourhood revitalization that can enhance the capacity of individuals and families to build and sustain strong, healthy communities." I learned more about this project during a visit to the community centre a few years later, which I'll tell you about shortly, but the public face of the ANC's efforts appears on a short video posted to YouTube that is eerily reminiscent of *Some People Have To Suffer*, as if time had stood still. The same pans of scum-filled ditches, dilapidated houses, nearby industry, the Pattullo Bridge; residents talking to the camera about the reactions of people when they find out "oh, you live down there," or about "houses that are scrapyard-looking"; a girl who informs us that "it stinks" and she'd like to have the ditches covered; a boy who says he wants "the mosquitos to go away." "I don't know," another guy says, "Bridgeview seems to be a forgotten community. But this little neighbourhood here has more community spirit than I've ever seen." The video culminates in the "action" taken by the community. A caption pops up: Outsiders routinely dump their garbage in Bridgeview, and we see several people with gloves, tongs, and yellow trashbags as a voiceover describes the swelling of their volunteer brigade to fifteen members, who collect enough trash to fill five dump trucks.

This is the community action, I think? "Animating" the residents to clean up the trash of people who look down their noses at them? I almost choke up, though, when one trash-picker looks into the camera, a glint in his eye: "We try to find out whose garbage it is, so we look at the stuff and see if we can find phone numbers," he confides. "We all have cellphones, so we can give them a call . . ."

Bridgeview has also attracted the attention of the Toronto-based Mammalian Diving Reflex (MDR), a "research-art atelier dedicated to investigating the social sphere, always on the lookout for contradictions to whip into aesthetically scintillating experiences." Founded in 1993 by artistic director Darren O'Donnell, the MDR operates through what it calls "'social acupuncture': playful, provocative, site and social-specific participatory performances with non-actors of all ages and demographics, designed to bring people together in new and unusual ways." O'Donnell and his team have gone to communities around the world (in Belgium, Germany, Australia, Ireland, Scotland, Denmark, and Japan, to name a few) and staged events like Haircuts by Children (exactly what it sounds like); the Children's Choice Awards, in which children adjudicate at arts festivals; or Eat the Street, where strangers are invited to have dinner with a group of children at a local restaurant, after which the kids write culinary reviews. As I looked over Mammalian's extensive website, it appeared that Bridgeview was the only locale in British Columbia to have been chosen for the MDR treatment. In 2012, for instance, Amy Fung reported on a recent Eat the Street event during Vancouver's PuSH Arts and Performance Festival, where "children in grades 5 and 6 from Bridgeview Elementary in Surrey have been appearing in restaurants throughout Gastown, taking notes of their dining experiences, from the décor of the washrooms to new foods tried." She praised the "underlying principle of the event," which lay in "the trust and communication between the children and the working members of MDR, who instilled agency into the children's hands and let them set the tone in a social situation where their opinions and wants are often ignored." It was "one of the best socially engaged practices" she had ever participated in.

In the summer of 2010 I showed up at the Bridgeview Community Centre for the annual Bridgeview Days event, hoping to find some old-timers I could interview about the Challenge for Change days. The hall was alive with the clamour of rambunctious kids, and I was offered my choice of refreshments: hotdogs on one table, and on another an extensive array of Indian dishes, home-cooked by the women of the neighbourhood. A man in a Sikh turban introduced himself to me, but it was so noisy I didn't catch his name. When I told him I wanted to speak with residents who were there during the '70s, he told me he was a relatively recent arrival, but that Bernadette Keenan, a longtime resident, would soon be arriving. She was to receive an award later in the day, he said, in appreciation for her work.

As I sat down at a table with my plate of daal and paneer, I noticed that most of the crowd was of South Asian descent — representative of the changing demographic in the neighbourhood and, indeed, in Surrey generally. Bernadette showed up, as well as another woman who had recently had to move out of the neighbourhood when her house was demolished for construction of the new South Fraser Perimeter Road (SFPR). This was, I knew, the latest battle for Bridgeview: protests, demonstrations, and sit-ins proliferated as attempts were made to keep this mammoth project from cutting a path of polluting trucks and cars through the community. I had been following their efforts on Facebook and blog posts, and Bernadette and I talked a little about the environmental impact of the SFPR, which was planned to run all along the south bank of the Fraser.

She and her friend seemed disgruntled about the Bridgeview Days festivities that year. For one thing, they should have been held a week earlier so as not to conflict with Whalley Days, which were happening up at Surrey Centre. I asked about the Action for Neighbourhood Change project: had they been a part of that? Yes, they had, though from their point of view it was something of a failure. So they had broken off, they said, and formed "Bridgeview in Motion." It was this splinter group, I gathered, that had spearheaded the cleanup days in the neighbourhood.

As though to get down to the nitty-gritty, the two women asked me if Bridgeview seemed "different" from what I remembered. There was something in their tone, their insinuating glances, that led me to suspect they were referring to the more diverse cultural makeup of the neighbourhood, and I gave a noncommittal answer. They then had a conversation between themselves about a recent community centre board meeting that had not been fully translated, so they couldn't follow what was being said. It was becoming apparent that Bridgeview was not one community but a number of communities, not necessarily bound together by their geographical proximity.

Just then a young woman sat down at the table, opened a lunch box she had brought, and took out a salad. She seemed as interested in my presence there as I was in hers, so we started a conversation. Maybe I asked her how long she had lived in Bridgeview, I'm not sure, but her answer sent a shiver of the uncanny through me. She wasn't a resident. She was a researcher.

"So am I," I told her, astonished to find my own presence there doubled in hers. Serena Kataoka had been coming to Bridgeview for over a year. She was working on a dissertation in political science at the University of Victoria, and Bridgeview was her case study. Had I seen the treasure trove of photos, binders, and other records in the community centre's office? No? We could go take a look later, she said, after the ceremony was over.

It had been too noisy to record any conversations to this point, and now the festivities were heating up. First, Serena was called to the front by one of the men who had greeted me when I came in — they seemed to be the main officiators of the event. Serena was asked to lead the kids in a race at the front of the hall. Then Bernadette was called up to cut the celebratory cake and receive her award. Next, to my surprise, I was called up to join the town fathers in handing out certificates and awards to worthy residents, most of them children. It was as though Serena and I were visiting dignitaries. Over and over again, a wrapped package was handed to Serena and a certificate to me, and we in turn presented these to the recipients, with a perfunctory handshake, as they came onstage. A photo was taken of each transaction. At the end, both Serena and I were asked to address the assembled audience, though I have no idea what I concocted for the occasion.

I was confused by my role there: was I a researcher, or was I a participant in Bridgeview's ongoing narration of itself? Are those photos now displayed in one of the binders locked away in the community centre's office, that office I never visited in the end, since the festivities had taken up most of the day, and Serena was suggesting that we decamp to a Starbucks up in Surrey Centre? Was Serena checking me out, the academic competition, an interloper where she had already established her credentials as the official scholar of Bridgeview and its woes? On the way up the hill (I gave Serena a ride in my rental car, feeling self-conscious for not having used public transportation as she had done) I obsessed a little bit about her lunch box: had I broken some unspoken researcher rules by partaking in the community centre's food rather than bringing my own fare?

Our coffee together was revelatory. First of all, the lunch box was only to ensure that Serena could eat gluten free — an expedient she often resorted to, nothing to do with some sort of research protocol. Turned out we had much to share with each other: reading suggestions, observations, the sense that there was something astonishing about how Bridgeview just kept attracting attention, from urban developers, from well-meaning do-gooders, from academic investigators like us. Although my focus was on the 1970s, I seemed nevertheless to be addressing some of the same phenomena that Serena was in her own work. Most surprising was that as we filled in the details of our personal pasts, we discovered that we were both partnered with women. What did that mean? Was urban politics the new cruising ground for lesbians? Were we engaged in the next phase of Queer Theory?

Later she shared with me an illuminating paper she had written about the intricacies of how the Action for Neighbourhood Change program had unfolded in Bridgeview, from which I will share just a snippet, so redolent is it of the Bridgeview of the 1970s.

> Bridgeview residents have a strong sense of community pride, in spite of being dumped on (literally, with garbage, and figuratively, with insults) by people from the rest of the Lower Mainland, and so they are focused on improving the physical infrastructure of the neighbourhood.

And what was it in particular about that "physical infrastructure" they wished to focus on? The manager of the ANC project had attempted at first to "engage Bridgeview residents in conversations relating to federal policies," but it was to no avail because "all they wanted to talk about was ditches. Bridgeview does not yet have a sanitary sewer system, and its streets are lined with open ditches."

What was this I was learning? That although Bridgeview had gotten its sewers in the late '70s, these sewers were now, in the 2010s, failing. It was time to start all over again.

Fast forward a few more years, and I see that while Surrey has authorized a new sewer system for Bridgeview, there are many in the community who are leery of its cost.

As well, the South Fraser Perimeter Road is a done deal. Early one morning, before the sun came up, I was in my rental car, driving from my brother's house to the airport, following the instructions of my GPS. It took me on the most efficient route, and despite my intention to boycott the highway that now slashes through Bridgeview, right where Otto's childhood house would have been, I found myself speeding along the SFPR anyway, too groggy to defy the matter-of-fact instructions of the automated voice guiding me through the dark.

And just today I checked in to see what one of the Bridgeview activists was up to, a woman I didn't meet in 2010 because she had gone to the Whalley Days event instead. There wasn't a lot of activity on Sonia's page, though I did notice that she had updated her profile picture back in 2015, putting up the image of a lovely leaf-lined path leading through a stand of evergreens to a lighted clearing in the distance. A friend calls it "very Thoreau" and thanks her for sharing. But Sonia informs her that this bit of park is "no longer." The SFPR now runs through it.

The Return of the Mudflats Shacks

And what of the Maplewood Mudflats? Were they filled in with concrete to give birth to the North Van District mayor's dream of a marina and a city centre? Though you would not know it from the conclusion of the films, with the squatters' shacks seeming to all go up in flames, it could be said that the people won out against "p-r-r-rogress" in the long run. My sense of what happened after the 1971 Christmas evictions is hazy. Mike Bozzer was allowed to stay, and some of the other residents say they returned in the mid-'70s to spend a little more time on the flats. North Shore news outlets ran stories of proposals for the site, but none of them ever came to fruition. Tom Burrows, as I've told you, divides his time, still making art, between Gastown and Hornby Island; Paul Spong has made the study and safeguarding of whales his life's work up on Hanson Island; Paul's former wife, Linda, and her husband, Bill Gannon, last I spoke with them, were tracking the progress of mammoth oil tankers through Vancouver's nearby waters, part of their "No Tankers" campaign. I talked to Roger Brewton down in Alameda, California, where he was just about to cut his long hair, which at fourteen or fifteen inches was "way more of a hassle" than he had remembered from his youth. He was going to donate it for kids with cancer. Dan Clemens, following in Lowry's tracks perhaps, runs the enchanting Hotel Casa Dan in Oaxaca, Mexico; John Dafoe is a guide and environmental consultant on the Sunshine Coast, where Ian Ridgway also lives. Ridgway continues to build in that mudflats style, though on a smaller scale, and is writing a book of his own on those squatting days.

Willie Wilson, Ian tells me, appears to be "making trouble" on Hornby Island. I couldn't find it, but there was an article Ian read, "saying that people were worried about all this stuff he was still collecting and it was just spilling out of his land. I'm sure it's just the usual tangle of collected objects," Ian said. "He was annoying his neighbours."

Meanwhile, in the final stages of writing this book, I was scrolling through the images of a plein-air painter I met a few years ago. Like me, Jeremy Herndl had been invited to the Surrey Art Gallery for a forum titled "Peripheral Visions: The Centrality of Landscape on the Fringe," which featured Jeremy's evocative renderings of outdoor spaces in Surrey. These images were redolent of the years I had lived there in the '70s: beyond a weather-beaten fence in his father's backyard, a darkening landscape is glimpsed through a stand of saplings, the lights on the far side of the Fraser winking between the trees; a ghostly denuded tree presides over an empty parking lot, a typical three-storey apartment building lurking in the background; ranked lights in a parking garage signal through spindly branches thrusting up from an anonymous, trash-strewn bit of soil. I was revisiting some of these paintings on Jeremy's online gallery when I happened on two images I hadn't noticed before. There were more trees, but these were lush with the green foliage of late spring. And beneath them, a jumble of rusting auto carcasses, tires, and other unrecognizable scraps of the industrial world. One painting was titled *Pacific Recycling*. The other?

Wepruk's Yard.

How had I not seen these paintings? I emailed Jeremy, sending him the entire section on Wepruk I had just composed.

Oh yes, Jeremy said. He had spent days working on those paintings around 2013 and had many a conversation with Matt, who told him all about his battles with City Hall.

Matt had become "exasperated by people living in the nearby woods," a veritable village of them, camping out in "squalor and addiction." They would come into his yard and rip off what copper wire or aluminum they could find to resell for a few bucks. "Matt took pride in his yard," Jeremy said, "and thought of it as kind of a museum, albeit in a pitiful state, and he appreciated the fact that I was painting it."

So even as Willie Wilson had become the Matt Wepruk of his

Hornby Island neighbourhood, Matt Wepruk had been dubbed, through the magic of Jeremy Herndl's paintbrush, a kind of Willie Wilson of Bridgeview.

The estuarial beach on the North Shore seems to have been left intact all these decades and is now the Maplewood Conservation Area, popular with bird watchers from far and wide. Whether it was the films depicting the squatters' concern for the environment or something else, Vancouver has been loath to destroy this little stretch of its foreshore treasures.

Curiously, if you go for a walk along the conservation area's wooded paths, you seem to catch a glimpse of the squatters' shacks from days of yore, reflected like ghosts in a pool of water among the trees. They were all burned or bulldozed decades ago, so how is it that three of them seem to have drifted back again to haunt the North Shore? The three ramshackle cabins are on stilts, finished with unpainted cedar shingles, bric-a-brac, and driftwood, their many-paned windows reflecting the late afternoon sun. Is it a hallucination? A mirage? Something seems off with the scale somehow.

It turns out that during Vancouver's most recent foray into the global limelight, when it hosted the 2010 Olympics, Ken Lum was one of several artists contracted to fashion public art installations that would run concurrently with the games. Working from photographs and the documentary films, Lum had three scale models built: one each of Malcolm Lowry's, Paul Spong's, and Tom Burrows's shacks, painstakingly reproducing almost every architectural detail down to the exact pitch of the roofs and the random plywood scraps reinforcing an exterior wall. I first saw the mini-shacks at their original downtown Vancouver installation site, a new public art venue for the Vancouver Art Gallery called "Off Site," where pedestrians hurried past, glancing over at the waist-high structures on a reflecting pool at the foot of the Shangri-La, Vancouver's tallest and most ostentatiously lavish new hotel. Titled *From Shangri-la to Shangri-la*, Lum's installation was meant at the very least to prompt a meditation on the contradiction between two senses of this term, originally coined by novelist James Hilton to refer to

'A kind of Willie Wilson of Bridgeview.' PACIFIC RECYCLING (MATT WEPRUK'S YARD) Jeremy Herndl; oil on canvas. 72cm x 62cm, 2013

his Orientalist vision of a hidden, enchanted utopia far off in the Himalayan mountains, where the ideal conditions for life lead to happiness and longevity. On the one hand, the Shangri-La Hotel itself represents the kind of sumptuous living conditions that only abundant capital, zoning and tax laws that favour corporate development, and international mobility can buy. On the other hand, the dwarfed and modest squatters' shacks point "back in time" but also to another ethic of living altogether, one made possible only by the renunciation of material abundance in favour of an almost ascetic "closeness" to nature — like a secular monastery. The accompanying text at the installation urges passersby to meditate on the historical specificity of the shacks, recounting the story of Lowry's Dollarton cabin and the Maplewood Mudflats settlement,

'A kind of vestigial memory.' Ken Lum, FROM SHANGRI-LA TO SHANGRI-LA. Installation at Off-Site, Vancouver Art Gallery, 2010

and stressing the "acute contrast between the rustic character of the shacks and the rigorously engineered mass of the nearby towers." The installation is not so much "an attempt to recover a lost Arcadian project or establish an overly-simplified duality between past and present," the text explains:

> *Considered in relation to the surrounding environment, the reproductions of these mudflat shacks appear as a kind of vestigial memory, traces from a foreclosed moment in the lower mainland's history that proposed a rustic perfection embodied in the surrounding architecture. In marking a history of diverging world views, they extend an invitation to consider the ongoing processes of idealization that shape our understandings of the city and the way citizens and community are constituted in the spaces these processes produce.*

A few months after the Olympics concluded, the shacks disappeared, making way for a new temporary installation. Eventually they were gifted by Lum to the District of North Vancouver, whose current mayor, Richard Walton (once a youthful visitor to the squatters' shacks in the '70s), recognized their value as visual reminders of the area's unique history. I can't decide, today, whether it is supremely appropriate or deeply ironic that the final venue turned out to be the Maplewood Mudflats. It doesn't seem to trouble anyone that Lum's title referencing the contrast of luxury high-rise to lowly shack, from Shangri-La to Shangri-La, will no longer make sense now that the replicas have been removed from their proximity to the towering hotel. But one thing's for sure: While squatting is no more tolerated on the North Shore now than it was in earlier decades, the simulation of squatting makes for good art.

Postscript

I opened this book with some lines from Woody Guthrie's folk tune "This land is my land, this land is your land," which we used to sing as kids. I never knew of the alternative version of the song penned by Pete Seeger until I saw it reproduced in a blog by Peter Bosshard, of International Rivers:

> *This Land is your land*
> *But it once was my land*
> *Until we sold you*
> *Manhattan Island*
> *You put our nations*
> *On reservations*
> *This land was stole*
> *By you from me.*

It is this stolen land that I was alluding to when I asked what hidden story might emerge from behind the squabbles over land use within a West Coast settler society that I was about to investigate — the hidden story that I related only a fraction of in the section on Len George's plans to put in a claim for the Maplewood Mudflats, or the section on Rhonda Larrabee's discovery of her Qayqayt ancestry.

Americans, and even most Eastern Canadians, may not be aware that in Vancouver and Victoria — Canada's largest West Coast cities — it has become customary to include in the opening remarks at public meetings, performances, school functions, art openings, and the like a statement along the lines of "We wish to acknowledge that our event today is taking place on the unceded (or traditional) territory of ..." and here the speaker identifies the First Nations people who lived there before colonialism, and still live there. For example, on the Surrey Art Gallery's website you will find the following announcement: "Surrey Art Gallery recognizes that our building is situated on the unceded traditional lands of the Salish Peoples including the Katzie, Kwantlen, Musqueam, Semiahmoo, Stó:lō, and Tsawwassen Nations."

This is a relatively recent phenomenon — or, rather, a recent mainstream practice, since it has long been routine for First Nations events, and even many events hosted by left-wing or socially conscious European-Canadians, to acknowledge the contested history of any given parcel of land in Canada. The first time I encountered this practice myself, some years before it began to show up in the mainstream, was when I attended that event on Occupy Vancouver at Rhizome Café in the Fall of 2011.

"While the specific terminology may vary," journalist Joshua Hergesheimer writes, "the underlying motivation is the same: an admission that the land we stand on belongs to those who lived here before colonization — those who made their homes along the shores and waterways of what we now call the Pacific Northwest."

While this is seen as empty lip service by many, the fact remains that a long-suppressed truth is being spoken, however belatedly, by the colonizers themselves. Before change occurs, a condition must be recognized. In this case, the condition is the fact that land was taken from those who for centuries had lived on it, taken care of it, and enjoyed its resources without depleting it, leaving almost no "carbon footprint" on it. The formal acknowledgement is only the first step in recognizing the importance of this land "along the shores and waterways" to the livelihood of Indigenous peoples on this continent.

'Reflected like ghosts in a pool of water.' Ken Lum, FROM SHANGRI-LA TO SHANGRI-LA, *now permanently installed in the Maplewood Mudflats conservation area.* Mike Wakefield, **North Shore News**

But why just the "shores and waterways"? Is this not true for all the land in British Columbia? For sure it is — but before the blanket deforestation of the lower Fraser Valley and the peninsula known today as "Vancouver," before the artificial drainage of all the low-lying areas to the south and east of the city, before the dykes and the dams, before the laying of thousands of miles of train tracks, before the skid roads, the paved streets, the cemented sidewalks finished with machine-extruded curbs — before the incremental encroachment that allowed massive settlement of all areas of what we now call the Greater Vancouver area, or the "Lower Mainland," human impact on this geographical part of the world remained limited to its shores and waterways, permitting, as they did, movement of small groups of humans in watercraft up and down the rivers and all along the coast, with only limited incursions into the mountains and the forests and places where water was not abundant. In other words, this saga of squatters' opposition to a culture of cement, and of a working-class neighbourhood's resistance to their City Hall's passion for development, was preceded by the more general story of the European displacement and annihilation of entire populations of First Nations peoples whose way of living was premised on moving with, rather than building a hardened crust over, the ebb and flow of periodic inundation.

It is not the place of this book to tell the innumerable stories of that history. But as I close this story I have told, of some of the contours of my own youth, I must at the very least acknowledge that these pages were researched, composed, and revised on the unceded or traditional territories of the Katzie, Kwantlen, Musqueam, Semiahmoo, Stó:lō, Tsleil-Waututh, Qayqayt, and Tsawwassen, not to mention the Narragansett, the Wampanoag, and the Penobscot Nations.

Notes

Forest Path to the Spring

"Pango Pango quality mingled with sausage and mash..." Malcolm Lowry, *Under the Volcano* (New York: New American Library, 1965), 126–27.

"At dusk, every evening..." "Thereafter at dusk..." "this is the time..." and all further quotes from Malcolm Lowry, "The Forest Path to the Spring," in *Hear Us O Lord from Heaven Thy Dwelling Place* (Philadelphia and New York: J.B. Lippincott, 1961), 215, 242, 259, 260.

"opened his arms, letting all the groceries fall..." Sheryl Salloum, *Malcolm Lowry: Vancouver Days* (Madeira Park, BC: Harbour Publishing, 1987), 31–32, 53.

"woman's blame..." Lowry, *Under the Volcano*, 63.

Surrey

"in the sewer ditch..." Salloum, *Malcolm Lowry*, 52.

"homeless homes with stoves..." Malcolm Lowry, *October Ferry to Gabriola*, ed. Margerie Lowry (New York and Cleveland: World Publishing Company, 1970), 5.

Mudflats

All references to the films taken from *Mudflats Living*, directed by Chris Paterson and Robert Fresco (National Film Board, 1972), 16mm film; and *Livin' on the Mud*, directed by Sean Malone (King Screen Productions, 1972), 16mm film.

"We couldn't own it..." Lowry, *October Ferry*, 325.

Curbs and Dykes

Vancouver Low Cost Street Program (video), Item #MI-27, City of Vancouver Archives.

"Heavy Rain Accentuates Deficiencies" and "Dams won't solve flooding problems," *Surrey–Delta Messenger*, August 23, 1973, and December 1973.

"When trees, vegetation and soils..." from "Re-inventing Urban Hydrology in British Columbia: Runoff Volume Management for Watershed Protection," on the Partnership for Water Sustainability in BC website (http://waterbucket.ca/cfa/files/2015/10/2003_Chicago-Conference_as-published.pdf), accessed September 4, 2016.

"Ditches play an important role..." from "Ditch Enclosures," on the City of Surrey website (http://www.surrey.ca/city-services/3644.aspx), accessed September 4, 2016.

In Suspension

"The mass-designed, mass-produced..." John Turner, "The Squatter Settlement: An Architecture that Works," in "Architecture of Democracy," special issue, *Architectural Design* (August 1968), 360 (http://www.communityplanning.net/JohnTurnerArchive/pdfs/ADAug1968SquatterSettlement.pdf), accessed September 4, 2016.

"Go placidly amid..." Max Ehrmann, "Desiderata," 1927.

For more on the Doukhobors, see Justine Brown, *All Possible Worlds: Utopian Experiments in British Columbia* (Vancouver: New Star Books, 1995).

"The shingled houses were falling…" Lowry, *October Ferry*, 177.

"To him fell the task…" Walter Benjamin, *Charles Baudelaire: A Lyric Poet in the Age of High Capitalism*, trans. Harry Zohn (London: Verso, 1983), 168–69.

Working on Oneself

"The squatter barriada-builder…" Turner, "The Squatter Settlement," 357.

"I could feel the improvement…" Lowry, "Forest Path," 231.

"I turned to Rex Weyler's substantial tome…" Rex Weyler, *Greenpeace: The Inside Story* (Vancouver: Raincoast Books, 2004), 205–14.

Drop-In

"Council had 'approved a recommendation…'" *Surrey–Delta Messenger*, June 3, 1971.

The Inter-Section story unfolds in the *Surrey–Delta Messenger*: "Directors Appointed for Inter-Section," June 11, 1970; "Crisis Center Opens Next Week," January 7, 1971; "Drop-In Bus a Mess," January 21, 1971; "Inter-Section Bus Busy," August 26, 1971; "1000 Calls in 10 Months Handled by Crisis Centre," November 25, 1971; "Crisis Centre Handled 1,323 Calls in December," January 27, 1972; "Bridgeview Offered Drop-In Centre for Local Teenagers," July 20, 1972.

"Because he himself had taken LSD…" For the Feldmar border story, see Linda Solomon, "LSD as Therapy? Write about It, Get Barred from US," in *The Tyee*, April 23, 2007 (https://thetyee.ca/News/2007/04/23/Feldmar/), accessed September 4, 2016.

For Andrew Feldmar's appearance on The Colbert Report, go to "Nailed 'Em — Northern Border," August 20, 2007, *Comedy Central* website (http://www.cc.com/video-clips/9a8i9h/the-colbert-report-nailed--em---northern-border), accessed September 4, 2016 (United States only).

"there's no knowing where it will all end," *Surrey Leader*, November 16, 1972.

"president of the Alcoholism Foundation of BC was quoted…" *Surrey-Delta Messenger*, June 3, 1971.

"Board Inspects Teen Dances," *Surrey Leader*, November 10, 1971.

Family

"The others… were all…" Lowry, "Forest Path," 221.

Extensions of the Family, directed by Kathleen Shannon (National Film Board, 1974), DVD.

Ram Dass, *Be Here Now* (San Cristobal, NM: Lama Foundation, 1971).

Bridgeview

For an account of the emergence of Bridgeview elementary school in 1949 see "The Development of Schools in Surrey 1940-1950," on the Surrey History website (http://www.surreyhistory.ca/schoolsto1950.html), accessed September 3, 2016.

Some People Have to Suffer, directed by Christopher Pinney (National Film Board, Challenge for Change Program, 1976), 16mm film.

Challenge for Change

For an excellent collection of essays on most of the Challenge for Change initiatives (excluding British Columbia) see Thomas Waugh, Michael Brendan Baker, and Ezra Winton, eds., *Challenge for Change: Activist Documentary at the National Film Board of Canada* (Montreal: McGill–Queen's University Press, 2010). For more on the Challenge for Change Surrey project see my article "Media Activists for Livability: An NFB Experiment in 1970s Vancouver," *Jump Cut* 54 (Fall 2012) (http://www.ejumpcut.org/archive/jc54.2012/JeanWaltonNFB/), accessed September 4, 2016.

"all land purchases and turnover . . ." Christopher Pinney, September-October Reports, Surrey Project, 1975, Douglas College Library Archives, New Westminster.

Shacking Up

On the Cecil Hotel see George Bowering, *Cars* (Toronto: Coach House Books, 2002); Janet Mackie, "Goodbye to Great Vancouver Nights at the Cecil Hotel," May 28, 2008, on the *Georgia Straight* website (http://www.straight.com/blogra/goodbye-great-vancouver-nights-cecil-hotel), accessed September 4, 2016; Weyler, *Greenpeace*, 209.

Return of Malcolm Lowry

"Round the point northwards . . ." Lowry, "Forest Path," 235.

Documentation for *Bridge Walk* can be found on Burrows's website (tomburrows.wordpress.com).

Otto Jr.

"Any plebiscite . . ." Surrey Council Minutes, July 27, 1970. Surrey is unusual in that the minutes of every council meeting ever held, from its beginning in 1880, are scanned and available on the Surrey Council website (http://www.surrey.ca/city-government/5515.aspx), accessed September 4, 2016. By contrast, I found that most other municipalities in Vancouver and the Lower Mainland have only made more recent council minutes available online.

Women's Lib

"the female chauvinist pig . . ." Bob Hunter, column, *Vancouver Sun*, December 10, 1971.

"a heightened awareness . . ." *Vancouver Sun*, December 30, 1971.

"Many of the people who attend these meetings . . ." from "Single Parents Become Targets of Vandals," *Surrey–Delta Messenger*, January 24, 1974.

"A girl in an office . . ." *Surrey–Delta Messenger*, February 4, 1971.

The Whorehouse

McCabe & Mrs. Miller, directed by Robert Altman (Warner Brothers, 1971).

"the town, all raw wood . . ." David Skerrit, ed., *Robert Altman: Interviews* (Jackson: University Press of Mississippi, 2000), 10–11.

"As the sets were being built . . ." Scott Watson, "Urban Renewal: Ghost Traps, Collage, Condos and Squats," on the Ruins in Process: Vancouver Art in the Sixties website (http://vancouverartinthesixties.com/essays/urban-renewal), accessed September 4, 2016.

"I'm a Cook"

I was crushed to discover that within a few months of our interview, Jackie Crossland died shortly after a diagnosis of cancer. A beautiful tribute to her by her partner, Nora Randall, can be found in the July 16, 2012, *Globe and Mail* (http://www.theglobeandmail.com/life/facts-and-arguments/jackie-crossland/article4420095/), accessed September 4, 2016.

Helen Simpson

Helen Simpson, "Mudflat Living," in *West Coast Song Book*, ed. Jim Brown (Vancouver: Blue Mountain Books, 1978), 26.

Bridgeview Residents

Adam Makos and Larry Alexander, *A Higher Call: An Incredible True Story of Combat and Chivalry in the War-torn Skies of World War II* (New York: Berkley Caliber, 2012).

"Franz Stigler and Charlie Brown BCTV 1997," CTV W-5 (https://www.youtube.com/watch?v=ZRKQvmT3Xhs), accessed September 4, 2016.

Land Claims, Whose Claims?

"I believe that the education . . ." from "You Can't Even Imagine How They Treated Us," interview with Rhonda Larrabee by Tereza Verenca, *New West Record*, June 9, 2015.

"the claim would be based on aboriginal rights . . ." from "Squatters Stop Bulldozer, Crew," *Vancouver Sun*, August 2, 1971.

Rhonda Larrabee's story can be found at "Reclaiming Roots: A Mother's Anguish Transforms a Painful History," on the Urban Systems website, February 13, 2014 (http://www.urbansystems.ca/reclaiming-roots-a-mothers-anguish-transforms-a-painful-history/), accessed September 4, 2016.

Relocation Schemes

"Bridgeview-in-the-trees . . ." from "Homes to Remain Bridgeview's Core," *Surrey Leader*, February 4, 1971. See also "Bridgeview Rejects Relocation," *Surrey–Delta Messenger*, May 10, 1973.

"faulty septic tanks are operating in the area . . ." Surrey Council Minutes, February 1, 1971.

"very friendly to the idea . . ." from "Bridgeview Residents Threaten Secession," *Surrey–Delta Messenger*, July 12, 1973.

"take over a recently vacated B.C. mining town . . ." from "Mud-Flat Squatters Make Offer to Move," *Vancouver Sun*, October 12, 1971.

For the story of Bralorne, see "Bralorne-Pioneer: Their Past Lives Here," on the Virtual Museum website (http://www.virtualmuseum.ca/sgc-cms/histoires_de_chez_nous-community_memories/pm_v2.php?id=exhibit_home&fl=0&lg=English&ex=00000470), accessed September 4, 2016.

"Gold Dust Twins Settlement Society" from "Squatters' Homes Bulldozed," *Vancouver Sun*, December 17, 1971.

"the ravines that run through Surrey . . ." from "Positive Youth Programs," *Surrey Leader*, March 25, 1971.

"the government messed that up for us too," from "Squatters' Homes Bulldozed," *Vancouver Sun*, December 17, 1971.

Stewards of the Environment

"as part of a unique and harmonious..." from "Burrard Haven Threatened by Concrete: Squatters Fear for Mud Flat Wildlife," *Vancouver Sun*, July 31, 1971.

"the red votive candle..." Lowry, *Hear Us O Lord*, 226.

"You've got Hooker Chemical..." Robert Sarti, "Mud Flats No Shanty Town," *Vancouver Sun*, July 27, 1971.

"the scattered folk who lived in [the cottages]..." Lowry, *October Ferry*, 64–65.

Scrap

"The owner is continually piling old wrecks..." Surrey Council Minutes, February 14, 1972.

"industrial use of warehousing..." Surrey Council Minutes, October 7, 1974.

"Highways Scenic Improvement Act..." Surrey Council Minutes, July 10, 1978.

"the accumulation of rubbish..." Surrey Council Minutes, August 14, 1978.

"Chief Inspector stated..." Surrey Council Minutes, June 11, 1979.

"the business was performing a service..." Surrey Council Minutes, June 5, 1967.

"One Legged Man Awarded," on the Narkive website (http://van.general.narkive.com/YF96iRXg/one-legged-man-awarded-280-000-in-damages-after-confronting-meth-heads-on-his-property), accessed September 4, 2016.

"barred from claiming income-related damages..." from "Jennifer Lee McGarva, et al. v. Dmetro (Matt) Wepruk" summary on Supreme Court of Canada website (http://www.scc-csc.ca/case-dossier/info/sum-som-eng.aspx?cas=31434&pedisable=true), accessed September 4, 2016.

"belligerent and less than cooperative..." from "Bhagaoti Prasad (Plaintiff) and Metro Wepruk (Defendant)" on the Animal Legal and Historical Center website (https://www.animallaw.info/case/prasad-v-wepruk), accessed September 4, 2016.

"Home Theme Spanish for Vander Zalms," *Surrey–Delta Messenger*, May 14, 1970.

Human Settlements

"The Livable Region..." Harry Lash, *Planning in a Human Way: Personal Reflections on the Regional Planning Experience in Greater Vancouver*, Urban Prospects series (Toronto: Macmillan, 1976), 54.

"What the people really seek..." from "Interview with Bill Vander Zalm," *Surrey–Delta Messenger*, January 30, 1975.

"Later this fall the Surrey Project..." Christopher Pinney, letter to L. Wallace, Deputy Provincial Secretary, October 16, 1974, Douglas College Library Archives, New Westminster.

"serve to improve the communities..." quoted in Sandra Came, "Urban Showdown: Watch Vancouver in 1976," *Universal Man* (May 1974), 29.

"With only five months' notice..." Lindsay Brown, "In Memory of Habitat Forum's Al Clapp," Habitat Forum 76 blog (http://habitat76.ca/2013/05/rip-al-clapp-february-1930-2013-habitat-forum/), accessed September 4, 2016.

"use unemployed people..." Joseph Roberts, "Alan Clapp Habitat '76," *Common Ground*, June 2006 (http://commonground.ca/OLD/iss/0606179/cg179_AlanClapp.shtml), accessed September 4, 2016.

"It was made out of salvaged yellow cedar..." Pete McMartin, "World's Longest Bar," *Vancouver Sun*, June 24, 2006.

"Under the banner of Habitat..." David Gurin, article in *Planners Network Newsletter* 6 (October 22, 1976), 3.

Details on the Group of 77 from Moira Farrow, "Land. That's What Habitat Was About," *Vancouver Sun*, June 23, 1976, 6.

References to the "New International Economic Order," *The Vancouver Declaration on Human Settlements* (1976), 2, 3, 8. Available on the UN Habitat website (http://unhabitat.org/wp-content/uploads/2014/07/The_Vancouver_Declaration_1976.pdf), accessed September 4, 2016.

"90% of all housing was constructed..." Enrique Peñalosa, quoted by Don Alexander, "Habitat '76, Thirty-five Years On," *Planning West* 53:3 (Fall 2011), 9.

For a list of the issues treated at Habitat, I consulted the inventory for the "Habitat Collection: (Association in Canada Serving Organizations for Human Settlements)" at the University of British Columbia Library Rare Books and Special Collections, prepared by Barbara Bohm (1977) and Margaret Ngwira (1978).

"Since 'private land ownership'..." *Vancouver Declaration*, 28–29.

"'every state' had the 'sovereign right to rule...'" *Vancouver Declaration*, 6.

"The Vancouver Declaration included..." Farrow, "Land. That's What Habitat Was About."

"Canada had 'sponsored the Habitat conference...'" Gurin, *Planners Network Newsletter*, 3.

"Residents of such 'unauthorized' settlements..." *Vancouver Declaration*, 27. For a much more detailed, and trenchant, account of Habitat and Habitat Forum, see Felicity D. Scott, *Outlaw Territories: Environments of Insecurity/Architectures of Counterinsurgency*, New York: Zone Books, 2016.

The Performative Art of Squatting

"I'm glad we did it ourselves..." "Squatter's Homes Bulldozed" and "Squatters Set Own Homes Ablaze," *Vancouver Sun*, December 17, 1971, and December 18, 1971.

"We noticed that the boundaries..." from Tom Burrows's website.

On self-help housing see John Turner and Robert Fichter, eds., *Freedom to Build* (London and New York: Collier Macmillan, 1973); Turner, *Housing by People: Towards Autonomy in Building Environments* (New York: Pantheon, 1977).

"The actual or threatened destruction of communities..." John Turner, article, *Planners Network Newsletter* 6 (October 22, 1976), 5.

"Fathy 'explained how to use local materials...'" Gurin, *Planners Network Newsletter*, 4.

Tom Burrows's "Skwat Doc" is in the collection of the Morris and Helen

Belkin Art Gallery at University of British Columbia. Documentation for "Skwat Doc" can be found on Burrows's website.

Bridgeview at Habitat

"brought by national and intergovernmental delegates..." Jacke Wolf, "Habitat — The Built World Speaks Its Mind," *The Rotarian*, (October 1976), 28–29.

"that any member of the T.V. media..." Surrey Council Minutes, June 21, 1976.

Bridgeview Today

The text of Bridgeview's historical placard is now also available on the City of Surrey website (http://www.surrey.ca/culture-recreation/2339.aspx), accessed September 4, 2016.

"learning initiative that explored..." from the "Surrey" section on the Action for Neighbourhood Change website (http://www.anccommunity.ca/Surrey.html), accessed September 4, 2016.

"a short video posted to YouTube..." *Bridgeview Today*, an Action for Neighbourhood Change-sponsored video (https://www.youtube.com/watch?v=9YozG-4fW2aw), accessed September 4, 2016.

"a research-art atelier..." from "About" on the Mammalian Diving Reflex website (mammalian.ca/about/).

"children in grades 5 and 6 from Bridgeview..." from "Eat the Street, Mammalian Diving Reflex" on the Post Specific Post website (http://postspecificpost.tumblr.com/post/16858160316/eat-the-street-mammalian-diving-reflex), accessed September 4, 2016.

"Bridgeview residents have a strong sense..." Serena Kataoka, "Politicizing Civil Cities: Bridgeview Community Building Initiatives" (unpublished manuscript, 2010), 18.

The Return of the Mudflats Shacks

Jeremy Herndl's ravishing plein-air paintings can be seen on his website (http://jeremyherndl.com/home.html), accessed September 4, 2016.

For the story of Lum's gift of the shacks to the District of North Van, see Jen St. Denis, "Squatters' Shacks now a Work of Art," *North Shore News*, August 10, 2012 (http://www.nsnews.com/news/squatters-shacks-now-a-work-of-art-1.347285), accessed September 4, 2016.

Postscript

Pete Seeger's version of "This Land Is Your Land," quoted in Peter Bosshard, "This Land Is My Land — Or Is It?" on the International Rivers website (https://www.internationalrivers.org/blogs/227/%E2%80%9Cthis-land-is-my-land%E2%80%9D-%E2%80%93-or-is-it), accessed September 4, 2016.

"The Surrey Art Gallery recognizes that..." Surrey Art Gallery website (http://www.surrey.ca/culture-recreation/13156.aspx), accessed September 4, 2016.

"While the specific terminology may vary..." Joshua Hergesheimer, "Unceded Territory," *Megaphone Magazine*, March 18, 2016 (http://www.megaphonemagazine.com/unceded_territory), accessed September 4, 2016.

Acknowledgments

Having dwelt temporarily in more than one generic district (in its guise as a "novel" and then a hybrid "memoir/histoire" as I called it at one point), this book has travelled a many-years' distance before finally settling in the overlapping territories of history and literary nonfiction. I thus owe deep gratitude to a long list of individuals and institutions who helped me along the way.

The University of Rhode Island generously came through with material support in the form of travel, research, and subvention grants, not to mention serving as the institutional version of the comfy shack in which much writing could happen: thanks in particular to the College of Arts and Sciences (especially Dean Winnie Brownell); the Harrington School of Communication and Media; the Center for the Humanities; the Department of English; and the Office of the Provost.

There would be no book, of course, if I hadn't been able to rely on the goodwill and trust of my many interlocutors. On the subject of the Maplewood Mudflats squats and the *McCabe & Mrs Miller* set, my deep gratitude goes to Roger Brewton, Tom Burrows, Dan Clemens, Jackie Crossland, John Dafoe, Bill and Linda Gannon (a.k.a. Tusi Spong), Allen Garr, Marshall Mar, Jim Munro, Ian Ridgway, and Paul Spong. On the subjects of Bridgeview and the Challenge for Change project in Surrey, I thank Baird Blackstone, Fred Calhoun, Valerie Heidecke, Serena Kataoka, Bernadette Keenan, Sonia Nazar, and Otto Wittenberg, Jr., as well as social animators and National Film Board of Canada associates Jan Clemson, Dave Driscoll, Jim Gillis, Mo Simpson, Jim Sellers, and Norma Taite.

I want to thank especially the makers of the films at the centre of this book, namely Christopher Pinney and his team for *Some People Have to Suffer* (NFB, 1976); Sean Malone and Ed Dupras for *Livin' on the Mud* (King Screen Productions, 1972); and Robert Fresco and Chris Paterson for *Mudflats Living* (NFB, 1972). For the evocative photography that gives this book its visual dimension, I thank David Wisdom, Michael de Courcy, Mike Wakefield, Sean Malone, and the team at Photofest. Special thanks goes to Jeremy Herndl for his moving rendition of Matt Wepruk's scrapyard museum. Jeremy's plein air paintings continue to haunt my own visual sense of Surrey past and present. When I was at my wits' end about how to include a cartographic element, Eric Leinberger came to the rescue with a map showing where most of the action took place. I'm grateful to Robin Mitchell Cranfield for doing justice to the memorable aesthetics of the mudflats shacks on the cover of the book.

For archival assistance, I am indebted to Scott Watson, Jana Tyner, and Teresa Sudeyko at the Morris and Helen Belkin Art Gallery at UBC; Denise Dale and Linda Rogers at Kwantlen Polytechnic University in Richmond; Pierce Smith, Kate Heikkila, and Chelsea Bailey at the Surrey Archives; Jordan Strom at the Surrey Art Gallery; and Colin Preston at the CBC Archives. I received technical help at crucial moments from Raymond Lee at Brainstorm Video, Kevin J. Hamilton at PVS Video, and Tony Balko at the URI Harrington "Hub."

For useful conversations in the overlapping domains of Canadian film studies, urban politics, and Vancouver in the '70s, I thank Lindsay Brown, Zoë Druick, Serena Kataoka, Randolph Jordan, Dave Murphy, and Thomas Waugh. Julia Lesage and the much missed Chuck Kleinhans recognized the importance of scholarship on the West Coast version of the Challenge for Change program, and published my article on it in *Jump Cut*.

I owe a special thanks to those who read (or heard) early versions of this project, and who kept it from dying on the vine before it ever reached the blossoming stage: Valerie Heidecke, Gwen Ashbaugh, Carolyn Betensky, Peter Covino, Amy Hoffmann, Roberta Stone, Caren McCourtney, Gabrielle Wellman, Sheri Wills, Jim Morrison, Justine Wiklo, Kim Hardy, Nancy and Jack Walton, and my agent, Malaga Baldi. I'm grateful to Rolf Maurer for giving the book a perfect dwelling place at New Star Books. And close to the finish line, my manuscript underwent the gentle yet hawk-eyed scrutiny of the best editor ever, Audrey McClellan.

I would never have had the courage to make this leap into the world of crossover writing without the warmth, encouragement, and perspicacity of the other members of our Providence West Side writing group: Karen Carr and Russell Potter. They listened to every sentence of every draft over a period of almost a decade, and helped keep alive the "voice" through which this dream of mudflats living could find its eventual literary form. And finally, my partner Mary Cappello, who shares with me in equal proportion life's mundane tasks and the pleasures of literary composition, has made every dwelling we inhabit a writer's shack extraordinaire.

Copyright Jean Walton 2018. All rights reserved. No part of this work may be reproduced, stored in a retrieval system or transmitted, in any form or by any means, without the prior written consent of the publisher or a licence from the Canadian Copyright Licensing Agency (Access Copyright).

NEW STAR BOOKS LTD.
newstarbooks.com • info@newstarbooks.com

No. 107 – 3477 Commercial St. 1574 Gulf Road, #1517
Vancouver, BC   Point Roberts, WA
V5N 4E8 CANADA   98281 USA

The publisher acknowledges the financial support of the Canada Council for the Arts and the British Columbia Arts Council.

Canada Council   Conseil des arts   BRITISH COLUMBIA
for the Arts   du Canada   ARTS COUNCIL
                                       An agency of the Province of British Columbia

Cataloguing information for this book is available from Library and Archives Canada, collectionscanada.gc.ca

Cover by Robin Mitchell Cranfield
Map by Eric Leinberger
Typesetting by New Star Books
Printed & bound in Canada by Imprimerie Gauvin
First printing, October 2018